Love Songs of World War Three

by

ADRIAN MITCHELL

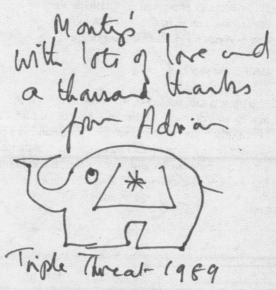

*Monty's —
with lots of love and
a thousand thanks
from Adrian*

Triple Threat 1989

Allison & Busby
Published by W. H. Allen & Co Plc

*(sorry Woman Overboard was
too late to get in this book!.)*

An Allison & Busby book
Published in 1989 by
W.H. Allen & Co. Plc
175/9 St. John Street
London EC1

Copyright © 1988 by Adrian Mitchell
Set by Phoenix Photosetting, Chatham, Kent
Printed and bound in Great Britain by
Cox & Wyman Ltd, Reading, Berkshire

ISBN 0 85031 991 9

DEDICATION

For my brother Jimmy, his wife Anne and their
children Ruth, Mark and Juliet, with love.

And for all who sang these songs.

ACKNOWLEDGEMENTS

Thanks are due to the following publishers who first published the books in which these songs appeared: Calder & Boyars (for *Marat/Sade* and *US*); Methuen (for *Tamburlane the Mad Hen*, *Man Friday*, *Mind Your Head*, *You Must Believe All This*, *The Tragedy of King Real* and *Animal Farm*); Jonathan Cape (for *Tyger*); Welfare State International (for *The Travels of Lancelot Quail*); Dramatic Publishing Co. (for *A Child's Christmas in Wales*); Oberon (for *The Pied Piper*); Ariel Music (for *The Last Wild Wood in Sector 88*) and Writers & Readers (for *Houdini*).

INTRODUCTION

In the days when everyone lived in tribes, poetry was always something which was sung and danced, sometimes by one person, sometimes by the whole tribe. Songs always had a purpose – a courting song, a song to make the crops grow, a song to help or instruct the hunters of seals, a song to thank the sun. Later on, when poetry began to be printed, it took on airs. When the universities started studying verse instead of alchemy, poetry began to strut around like a duchess full of snuff. By the middle of the twentieth century very few British poets would dare to sing.

*

There's a natural hunger for songs. The enormous popularity of good musicals and some bad musicals underlines this. But there's no reason why the lyrics of a song shouldn't be good.

*

There's often a difference between some poems and some lyrics. Lyrics tend to be less concentrated, partly because they have to work instantly and partly because they must allow room for the music to breathe, some work for the music to do.

*

I've been very lucky in my composers. My working method is usually this. To discuss with the composer what songs are needed. To write lyrics and read them aloud to the composer – just to indicate tone, possible rhythms and make the meaning of the lyric clear. I may rewrite at this point if the composer has good suggestions. Then I hand over the lyrics and go write some more. Often I've had to write to very tight deadlines. The only short cut I've ever found in these circumstances, and I've used it very rarely, is to write lyrics to an existing tune and fail to inform the composer. I did this, for example, with Charlotte Corday's waltz in *Marat/Sade* which I wrote to the tune of *The Blue Danube* (not included in this book).

*

To explain my title. I was born on October 24th 1932, so I was a kid during World War Two. I believe that World War Three began in 1945 when we dropped the atomic bomb on Hiroshima. That war has been continuing ever since, in Malaysia, Aden, Vietnam, Zimbabwe, Czechoslovakia, Cyprus, Kenya, Suez, Hungary, Israel, Nicaragua and so on. The hope must be that it won't escalate. So all my songs have been written in wartime and they probably reflect it. And they are love songs because the main motive for writing them is love – the love of words, the love of listening to songs, the love of my family and friends for whom I write the songs and love for this poor planet and its living inhabitants, human and otherwise. But how the hell did I find myself writing plays with songs in a century like this? I've been bloody lucky, as you will see.

*

My mother loved the theatre and she took me to almost any play or show I wanted to see. Every season we would visit the Gilbert and Sullivan operas. I memorised most of W. S. Gilbert's lyrics, which I found endlessly funny and clever.

*

The big American musicals knocked me sideways. *Oklahoma!* came first. I still think *The Surrey With The Fringe On Top* one of the sweetest love songs which never mentions love and *I Cain't Say No* one of the funniest point numbers. *Annie Get Your Gun* I liked even better at the time, though it hasn't lasted so well. I was still in love with Broadway musicals when *Pal Joey* and *The Pajama Game* proved that they don't have to be sentimental. And then *Guys And Dolls* — one of the greatest theatre pieces of all time, ranked alongside *The Beggar's Opera* for its combination of daring plot, character, wit, sharp lyrics and perfect music. But mostly, despite *Sweeney Todd*, the Broadway product is mindless, toothless and self-regarding. The star descends a staircase to be greeted by a Hello Dollying chorus, an eternally recurring image. . . .

As a teenager in the late Forties I was eccentric in my hobby — collecting records. Louis Armstrong, Danny Kaye, Dinah Shore, Duke Ellington, Fats Waller, Bing Crosby — whenever I could afford them, I bought them. At that time only about one in fifty teenagers shared this fascination. I even bought the *Melody Maker* along with the *New Statesman*, and from the MM, at the age of fourteen, learned for the first time about the extent of racism in the USA and the fact that it was growing in Britain.

*

And I listened to the words of the songs. The standard hit song of the time was full of abstract words like devotion and emotion plus a few property moons and stars above — awful lyrics like tons of white mud. But the blues was full of concrete images — *Make me a pallet on your floor, If you see me comin', sash your window high* or *I went down to St James Infirmary, saw my baby there, laying on a long white table, so sweet, so cold, so bare*. It was true poetry and I knew it.

*

Some of the funny songs of the period like *Talahassee* or *Accentuate the Positive* were good and witty. The old music hall songs often had flair and imagination. But at that time very few British poets were writing songs. Auden did some and Mac-Neice as well. But why weren't Dylan Thomas and George Barker writing lyrics for Duke Ellington to set?

*

Then came rock 'n' roll and the lyrics changed drastically as Tin Pan Alley was invaded by the forces of rhythm and blues. *Blue Suede Shoes, Heartbreak Hotel, Great Balls of Fire, Blueberry Hill, Sweet Little Sixteen* – they were jumping with images of city life.

*

Chuck Berry's songs were heady with the fumes of fast cars and cheap perfume. They told rapid-fire stories – *Come On, Maybelline* and, most amazing of all, *The Promised Land* in which the singer tells of an extraordinary cross-country journey from Virginia to Los Angeles with accidents thrown in.

*

But my favourite song-writing combination of that era was the team of Jerry Leiber (lyrics), Mike Stoller (music) and The Coasters. The best Coasters records – *Riot In Cell Block Number Nine, Searchin', Yakety Yak, The Shadow Knows, What About Us?, Little Egypt, Shopping For Clothes* and *D.W. Washburn* all seem to be sung by real people with real characters. Many of them, like *What Is The Secret Of Your Success?* are three-minute dramas with more than one character. Why is there no boxed set of the complete Coasters?

*

Leiber/Stoller went on to write many fine songs, especially for Peggy Lee – you may know *Is That All There Is?* but you should hear her extraordinary dark Leiber/Stoller LP called *Mirrors* which includes the wild version of *Professor Hauptmann's Performing Dogs*.

*

Along came the Beatles and suddenly British singers were writing their own lyrics. As their confidence grew, they pushed back the frontiers of lyric writing to achieve wonders like *Penny Lane, Come Together* and *A Day In The Life*. If you asked me, I could write a book. But onward. After the break-up, John Lennon stripped down his style to write some of the greatest lyrics ever in songs like *Mother*. This was naked poetry, frightening and true.

*

Since then many fine lyric writers have come and gone. The ones I have followed most avidly have been Paul Simon, Randy Newman and Bob Dylan. Lately I've been impressed with a lot of Elvis Costello, Sting and Peter Gabriel.

*

I'd love to write for singers like Joe Cocker or Madeline Bell, but somehow it never happened. Although I spent a couple of years writing about pop records, I concentrated on the lyrics and the beat and avoided as far as possible the sort of party contacts with the salesforce which you need to become a regular wordsmith.

*

In the past ten years I've been writing far fewer poems than I used to, mainly because most of that energy goes into my songs. Poetry is a bucket for carrying truth, and so are songs. I'm happy enough if I've got a bucket.

*

I'd started writing plays at the age of nine or ten. My school-master, Michael Bell, asked us to write an essay one day called *The Animals' Brains Trust*. Being awkward, I wrote a play instead. He sent me off to do the shopping in the nearby village. When I came back the other boys acted my play for me. And we performed it at the end of term for our parents. Michael couldn't have given me a greater present. It gave me my first taste of the satisfaction of having my work performed and enjoyed.

*

At my next school, Dauntsey's in Wiltshire, I met my greatest friend, Gordon Snell. The school ran an annual one-act play competition – you had to write your own – and the winning play won points for its House. Gordon and I collaborated on several of these plays. There was *A Friend Of Ours* in which a per-sonified Death (in a wheelchair) invited a group of people to his country house. There was a blank verse melodrama in which I had to say: "This bullet in my stomach is my life's result, The culmination of the sequence of my acts . . ." There was *The Third Ham* – a parody of *The Third Man* – which was banned by the school censors because of blasphemy and obscenity. Gordon and I took turns to direct and star in these dramas. One term he was playing Hamlet in the school play and I was Claudius, so we were barred from taking speaking parts in our last play. Thus we came to write *Cow Cow Bogey* – a western epic entirely centred round a Charlestoning cow, played by Gordon and myself. But we didn't include songs in our plays. Song-writing started, for me, at Oxford, contributing parodies of pop songs to an anti-Royal, anti-establishment revue called *Bad Taste*.

*

I became a journalist – a reporter on the *Oxford Mail* and also its theatre reviewer. I began to learn about the use of songs in non-Broadway theatre. Joan Littlewood's Theatre Workshop was my delight. And I began to understand the song theatre of

Brecht and, later, of John Arden.

*

I became committed to the idea of plays with songs, as opposed to musicals. I didn't want enormous budgets and compulsory, meaningless chorus lines. I didn't want songs designed for the hit parade rather than for dramatic effect, songs which had to be endlessly plugged in the show. What I wanted was *O What A Lovely War*, Behan's *The Hostage*, Alan Plater's *Close the Coalhouse Door*, John McGrath's *The Fish In The Sea* and Brecht's *The Caucasian Chalk Circle*. What I wanted was the kind of music theatre which Alan Dosser created at the Liverpool Everyman and Richard Eyre at Nottingham Playhouse, both directors in the Littlewood tradition. Eventually I worked with both of them.

*

The rest of my life in theatre, so far as it's relevant to the lyrics which follow, is contained in the introduction to each section. I've left out hundreds of songs, usually because they are meaningless outside their dramatic context. I've left out whole song shows for the same reason.

*

The greatest problem in staging most of the shows that follow has been that British theatres aren't geared to plays with songs. Musicians have to be specially hired, and, at nearly all rehearsals, you only have the pianist. Sound systems are usually rusty and unreliable. Actors have to be auditioned endlessly and exhaustively. I've learned never to believe actors who say they can sing (or actors who say that they can't).

*

What we need is a National Song Theatre. It will have a regular company of versatile musicians and actors who can all sing and dance. It will have several auditoriums with sound systems to equal those of rock groups. It will revive the best of music theatre from the past. It will create new plays with songs, both big and small. It will import music theatre from other countries, not just from the USA. It will constantly keep a touring company on the road. It will run its own theatre school. It will be built in Liverpool or Glasgow in the year 2024.

*

I enjoy my work tremendously. If I ever feel I should take on a project because it's a worthy cause, I consult GASTODAY, a theatre company which I formed in my head. GASTODAY stands for Glory And Song Theatre Of Daft Adventures Yes and its board has the power to prevent me from working on any project with which will be no fun. It can be a serious story, but I have to be able to fight with a light heart. Please sing along:

> G is for the Glory of the Golden
> A is And and Amazing Animal Arts
> S the Song that Soars like Buddy Bolden
> T's the Theatre with a Thousand Moving Parts
> O is Of and Open up Old Stories
> D is Daft and likewise the Reverse
> A's Adventures with a rousing Chorus
> Yes Yank them all together they spell
> GASTODAY – GASTODAY GASTODAY
> All my troubles seemed so far away –

And GASTODAY just turned down the job
Of Ruling the Multi-Verse

*

I don't want to make any claims for the lyrics which follow except that they were the best I could do, I think they are worth reading and that I'll try to do better in the future. I would like to thank all my collaborators – composers, fellow-writers, actors, directors, choreographers, designers, lighting and sound people, stagehands, stage management, producers, publicists and reviewers. And my family and friends for coming to these shows and singing along.

CONTENTS

INTRODUCTION   vii

THE LEDGE   1
His Aria   2
Her Aria   3

MARAT/SADE   4
Charlotte Corday's Arrival In Paris   6
Four Years He Fought   7
The People's Reaction   8
Copulation Song   8
Poor Old Marat   8
Final Song   9

US   10
Icarus Shmicarus   12
Any Complaints?   12
Zapping the Cong   13
Stimulating Song   15
When Dreams Collide   16
Moon Over Minnesota   17
Make And Break   19
To Whom It May Concern   20

THE HOTPOT SAGA   22
Victory March Song   24
Love Duet   24
Maximum Security Girl   25

Clobber A Copper   27
Ride The Nightmare   28

MOVE OVER, JEHOVAH or THE MAN WHO SHOT
EMILY BRONTE   30

Lullaby for Moses   32
The Violent God   32

LASH ME TO THE MAST!   34

Hungry Song   36
The Hairy Men From The Hills   37
Calypso's song to Ulysses   37

TAMBURLANE THE MAD HEN   38

It's a Smashing Feeling   39
Tamburlane Rock   40

TYGER   41

A Man May Be Happy   43
The Children of Blake   43
Randy Women's Song   44
Quintet Song   45
Happy Birthday William Blake   47
Poetry   48

MAN FRIDAY   49

Friday Begins His Story   51
Friday's Football Song   51
Friday's Swimming Song   52
Master And Friday   52
Friday's Song of Light   53
There Was A Man   53
The Tribe   54

MIND YOUR HEAD   55

Heaven Is a Hill Called Hampstead   56
Wash Your Hands   57
The Stone-Ground Freak Song   58

Never Stops   60
The Worst Thing   61
Bad Friday   61
Marie Lloyd   64
The Bum-Collector's Song   65
Marry Your Mother   65

KARDIFF RULES, OK?   66

Che Ballad   68
Schoolroom Song   69
Boogie To Bits   70
Try To Be More Like Margaret Thatcher To Look At   72

THE FINE ART OF BUBBLE-BLOWING   73

When One Dog Meets another   74
South Sea Bubble Song   74
My Three Sons   75
The Eighteenth Century Con-Man's Apology   75

TOTAL DISASTER   76

Lullaby to be sung by Security Officers   78
Ocean Liner Good Advice Song   78
Final Finale   79

THE FREE MUD FAIR   80

Gardening   82

A SEVENTH MAN   83

The Mother's Song   84
Peasant Song   85
The Weighing Machine   86
Factory Song   87
Bus Station   88
Medical   88
Song About Migrant Workers   89
The Gold   89
Day Off   90
The Workers   90

ROUND THE WORLD IN EIGHTY DAYS   92

What He's Not   93
The Reform Club   94
Dream Travel   95
The Song Of The Stokers   97
Elephant Song   98
English Lovers   99
Poppy Juice   100
Chinese Typhoon   101
Hotel Verandah   102
The Long Noses   103
Judy's Song   105
Pineapple Moon   106
The Happy-Go-Lucky Miners of San Francisco   107
Gold Rush Blues   108
Civilise This Land   110
Sandbank Song   111

HOUDINI   113

After-Life   115
Money Is The Only Medicine   115
A Song Of Liberation   116
The Police Force Of The World   117
Medicine Show Song   118
The First Journey   119
Speedwell   120

UPPENDOWN MOONEY   121

Song In Space   123
The Woman of Water   123
Love In A Nest   124
To A Postman   124
Shjom   125
The Squire's Curse   125
Belly Slapping Dance   126
Someone At My Door   127
Hush Little Baby   127
We've Got Pride   128

Late Afternoon   128

THE WHITE DEER   130

Doves And Roses   131

PEER GYNT   132

Great White Stallion   134
Me First (Troll Song)   135
Cutting Down The Tree   138
I Travelled On Skis   139
I Shall Survive   139
I Locked The Door   140
King Apis   141
The Emperor of Self   143
The Pig Song   143
The Song of the Thoughts   144
Sleep and Smile   145

MOWGLI'S JUNGLE   147

The Widow's Song   148

SOMETHING DOWN THERE IS CRYING   149

Something Down There Is Crying   150
Sorry Bout That   150

YOU MUST BELIEVE ALL THIS   155

You Must Believe All This   156
Not A Very Cheerful Song I'm Afraid   157

THE WILD ANIMAL SONG CONTEST   158

When The Eagle Smiles   160
The Dancing Bear   161
The Cameleopard   162
Rogan The Lion's Roaring Song   163

THE TRAVELS OF LANCELOT QUAIL   165

The Wondrous Genealogy of Lancelot Quail   166

The Boasting Song of Lancelot Quail   167
The Garden Party Song   168
Farewell Song   169

Voyage Song In Quest of the Mermaid Morwena   169
The Riddle At The Crossroads   171
Lament For The Welsh Makers   171
The Owl Song   175

ASTERIX AND THE GREAT DIVIDE   176

Wedding Song   177
Obelix Song   177
Roman Marching Song   178
Gaul's Song   178

A CHILD'S CHRISTMAS IN WALES   180

The Soft Snow Falls All Around   182
Oh, Christmas Means Pudding   184
Shining Heart   184
The Tell-A-Tale Song   185

RAISING THE TITANIC   187

She's Fine Fine Fine   188
Unthinkable Song   189
The Menu   190

THE TRAGEDY OF KING REAL   193

I Saw A Vision   194
King Real   194
Gonilla's Song   195
The Dance of the Keys   196
Claudella's Song   197
Party Games   198
Adderman's Song   199

C'MON EVERYBODY   201

The Truth   202
Ode To Her   203

New Skipping Rhymes   204
Fifteen Million Plastic Bags   205

ANIMAL FARM   207

Sugarcandy Mountain   209
Twenty-Seven Ribbons   209
Boulder Song   211
The Green Flag   212
Nothing Song   213
The Runt of the Litter   214
I See The Future   215

GREENHAM COMMON   217

Power To The People   218
Killer Submarine   219
A Hard Day's Night   220
A Little Help From Our Friends   221
Picket For Peace   222

ON THE LOOSE   224

Angel Water   226
Blue Cotton   228
Blues and Kisses   229

THE PIED PIPER   231

River Water   233
Rat It Up   234
Patchwork Rap   236
Gorgonzola Moon   237
Gone Missing   238
Secret Country   239

THE LAST WILD WOOD IN SECTOR 88   241

The Kids Object   242
Green   243

WE   245

Lovers Come, Lovers Go   246

His Hands   247
The Hymn of Unanimity   248
Lament For The Jazz Makers   249
Apeshit   250
Lilies of the Valley   252
Gather Together   253
The Hen and the Eagle   254
Evenings of Fire and Snow   255

LOVE SONGS OF WORLD WAR THREE   257

Victor Jara of Chile   259
The Biggest Bang   261
Just A Little Too Loud   262

THE LEDGE

It was my first job in professional theatre. Richard Rodney Bennett wanted a libretto for a one-act opera about a man on a ledge threatening to commit suicide. Why not?

I did my best. A policeman and a priest both failed to talk the man down. Eventually he decided to live after his wife managed to make him laugh. Unfortunately nobody understood how this laugh could be the dramatic turning point. I meant it to say that humour can be a restoration of balance.

(I remember sitting many times on top of a double-decker bus, planning different suicides. But I'd have to leave a note. And what would it say? I would start to write these notes in my head, mentally rewriting them and then catch myself thinking – I wonder if anyone'll publish it? And then laughing at myself on top of that red bus, stupidly worrying about the literary merits of my suicide note.)

Anyway, at that time I didn't have the understanding to realise the obscurity of my Saved By The Giggle theory. Sorry, Richard.

Composer: RICHARD RODNEY BENNETT.

Performed: Sadler's Wells Theatre, 1961

HIS ARIA

When the general proceeds down the lines of the wounded
In this hospital of a world,
The wounded lie to attention.
Any complaints? Any complaints?
Only the dying man dares to speak:
I am too afraid to sleep,
Scared to lose sight of the tea-mug on my locker.
Yes sir, I have a complaint.

If I could tell you
Why the ice grows hourly in my chest.
If I could tell you,
I would have no complaint.
If I could see straight
I would tell you the same as everyone else.
If I could walk straight
I would go the same way . . .

I know the simple, men and women
With eyes the colour of the sky.
Fear is something they read about.
They are so simple
Like a glass of water.
They can easily be swallowed
Like a glass of water.

HER ARIA

The body is a house, it is a tall one.
From the eyes you can see far.
I fit my body and control my hands.
The body is a house, a tall one.

This is my body, it can do good things,
Though without wheels or wings.
When it grows dark, this body,
I sleep calmly, breathing slowly.

This body is a house
That is not locked.

MARAT/SADE

In 1964 Peter Brook asked me to transform a literal translation of Peter Weiss's *The Persecution and Assassination of Jean-Paul Marat As Performed By The Inmates Of The Asylum Of Charenton Under The Direction Of The Marquis De Sade*. He chose me because the whole play is in verse – blank verse, couplets and songs – and a poet was needed. I was recommended by two separate friends as a poet who was interested in the theatre.

I was given the literal translation only ten days before rehearsals started, so I had to work desperately to turn out a possible first draft. It was an exciting and terrifying period. Attending every rehearsal, I saw Glenda Jackson's Charlotte Corday develop from initial strength into greatness. I watched Brook allowing his company to experiment, letting them develop different interpretations and only making his choice among them when the cast were bursting for leadership.

During rehearsals the New York composer, Richard Peaslee, would be at a piano in the back room at the Donmar, turning out new tunes which he would offer us once or twice a day. Every evening I would go home to rewrite and have a few nightmares.

The shortened title came about because when two reporters collaborate on a story they head their page with their names thus: Hazlitt/Cameron. So I took to heading my pages Marat/Sade and it stuck.

The night before *Marat/Sade* opened at the Aldwych, Peter told us solemnly that we should expect terrible reviews. Of course it was a hit, both in London and New York. The odd thing was that while the American critics and public reacted very much to the play's political references – to the civil rights stuggle and the war in Vietnam particularly, the London critics ignored its politics and concentrated on its thrilling theatricality.

Composer: RICHARD PEASLEE.

Performed: Royal Shakespeare Company, Aldwich Theatre, London. 1964.

Published: Calder and Boyars, 1964.

CHARLOTTE CORDAY'S ARRIVAL IN PARIS

Charlotte Corday came to our town
heard the people talking saw the banners wave
Weariness had almost dragged her down
Weariness had dragged her down

Charlotte Corday had to be brave
she could never stay at comfortable hotels
Had to find a man with knives to sell
had to find a man with knives

Charlotte Corday passed the pretty stores
Perfume and cosmetics powders and wigs
unguent for curing syphilis sores
unguent for curing your sores

She saw a dagger its handle was white
walked in through the cutlery seller's door
When she saw the dagger the dagger was bright
Charlotte saw the dagger was bright

When the man asked her who is it for
it is common knowledge to each one of you
Charlotte smiled and paid him his forty sous
Charlotte smiled and paid forty sous

Charlotte Corday walked alone
Paris birds sang sugar calls
Charlotte walked down lanes of stone
through the haze from perfume stalls
Charlotte smelt the dead's gangrene
Heard the singing guillotine

Don't soil your pretty little shoes
The gutter's deep and red
Climb up climb up and ride along with me
the tumbrel driver said
But she never said a word

never turned her head

Don't soil your pretty little pants
I only go one way
Climb up climb up and ride along with me
There's no gold coach today

But she never said a word
never turned her head

FOUR YEARS HE FOUGHT

Four years he fought and he fought unafraid
sniffing down traitors by traitors betrayed
Marat in the courtroom Marat underground
sometimes the otter and sometimes the hound

Fighting all the gentry and fighting every priest
businessman the bourgeois the military beast
Marat always ready to stifle every scheme
of the sons of the arse-licking dying regime

We've got new generals our leaders are new
They sit and they argue and all that they do
is sell their own colleagues and ride on their backs
and jail them and break them or give them all the axe

Screaming in language that no man understands
of rights that we grabbed with our own bleeding hands
when we wiped out the bosses and stormed through the wall
of the prison they told us would outlast us all

Marat we're poor and the poor stay poor
Marat don't make us wait any more
We want our rights and we don't care how
We want a revolution NOW

THE PEOPLE'S REACTION

Why do they have the gold
Why do they have all the power
Why do they have friends at the top
Why do they have jobs at the top
We've got nothing always had nothing
nothing but holes and millions of them
Living in holes
Dying in holes
Holes in our bellies
and holes in our clothes

Marat we're poor and the poor stay poor
Marat don't make us wait any more
We want our rights and we don't care how
We want our Revolution NOW

COPULATION SONG

And what's the point of a revolution
without general general
copulation copulation copulation

POOR OLD MARAT

Poor old Marat they hunt you down
The bloodhounds are sniffing all over the town
Just yesterday your printing press
was smashed now they're asking your home address

Poor old Marat in you we trust
You work till your eyes turn as red as rust
But while you work they're on your track
The boots mount the staircase the door's flung back

Marat we're poor and the poor stay poor
Marat don't make us wait any more
We want our rights and we don't care how
We want our revolution NOW

FINAL SONG

And if most have a little and few have a lot
you can see how much nearer our goal we have got
We can say what we like without favour or fear
and what we can't say we can breathe in your ear

And though we're locked we're no longer enslaved
and the honour of France is eternally saved
The useless debate the political brawl
are over there's one man to speak for us all
For he helps us in sickness and destitution
he's the leader who ended the Revolution
and everyone knows why we're cheering for
Napoleon our mighty Emperor

Led by him our soldiers go
Over deserts and through the snow
A victory here and a victory there
Invincible glorious and always victorious
for the good of all people everywhere

Charenton Charenton
Napoleon Napoleon
Nation Nation
Revolution Revolution
Copulation Copulation

US

In 1966 Peter Brook assembled a group to create a piece of theatre which would comment on the Vietnam War – as seen from England. The first group included Charles Wood the playwright, Albert Hunt the amazing director and teacher from Bradford College of Art, the designer Sally Jacobs, Michael Kustow, the American composer Richard Peaslee and myself. At an early stage Charles had to drop out and Denis Cannan joined the group in his place.

The process of making the show has been exhaustively described in the book *US* which is published by Calder and Boyars. I'd add to that book only a few comments.

The group writing process finally broke down because there was too great a split between the socialist and anarchists on one side and the liberals on the other. While the first act, whatever its inadequacies, did concentrate on the war itself, the second act became a domestic drama about an English woman trying to dissuade an Englishman from burning himself as a protest against the war – a drama which was extremely powerful but employed some specious arguments and seemed like an evasion of the war itself and Britain's responsibility for it.

I have a hundred reservations about the show, but I believe it was better than doing nothing and it did stimulate others to make public statements through the arts.

There were many problems. A rich guy offered to fly us all out to Vietnam to see for ourselves. Unfortunately he withdrew his offer after finding out that some of us had

10

already declared ourselves opposed to the American intervention/invasion.

We were still working under censorship. The Lord Chamberlain tried to ban the show outright for being "bestial, anti-American and communist", but the Governors of the Royal Shakespeare Company and Peter Hall helped Peter Brook to defeat that one and the show went on at the Aldwych.

People with short memories sometimes wonder why British artists ever imagined they could have any influence on the war. At that time there was pressure from the US as well as from intellectuals like Kingsley Amis and Bernard Levin for British troops to be sent to fight alongside the Americans. If the British anti-war movement did nothing else, it squashed that one flat.

Composer: RICHARD PEASLEE.

Performed: Royal Shakespeare Company, Aldwych Theatre, London. 1966.

Published: Calder and Boyars, 1967

ICARUS SHMICARUS

If you never spend your money
you know you'll always have some cash.
If you stay cool and never burn
you'll never turn to ash.
If you lick the boots that kick you
then you'll never feel the lash,
and if you crawl along the ground
at least you'll never crash.
So why why why-
WHAT MADE YOU THINK YOU COULD FLY?

ANY COMPLAINTS?

My girl Kate's teaching in the States,
Lecturing from town to town.
Pays her bills by, gets her thrills by
Studying the influence of Yeats on Yeats –

(CHORUS)
What's wrong with that?
What's wrong with that?
That's what she always wanted to be.
What's wrong with that?
If it makes her happy,
If it keeps her happy,
That's all that should matter to me.

My son Dave says he's living in a cave,
Hiding from the MI5.
Rank outsider, full of cider,
Goes to demonstrations for a good old rave.

12

(CHORUS)

My son Pete has a passion for defeat,
Never leaves the Twilight Zone.
He's a chronic melancholic
Chewing tranquillizers while he sits and sits.

(CHORUS)

My son Tom sends chatty letters from
Where they make pneumonic plague.
Scientific, feels terrific
Breeding germs to go into the Black Death Bomb.

(CHORUS)

My name's Adrian Mitchell and I like a bit of asymmetry
around the place so that's why verse three, as you'll have
noticed, has a fouled-up rhyme scheme, more fun that
way and-

What's wrong with that?
What's wrong with that?
That's what I always wanted to do.
What's wrong with that?
If it makes me happy,
If it keeps me happy,
That's all that should matter to you.

ZAPPING THE CONG

I'm really rockin' the Delta
From coast to coast.
Got em crawling for shelter,
Got em burning like toast.
And the President told me
It wouldn't take long,

But I know I'm in Heaven
When I'm Zapping the Cong.

Zapping the Cong
Back where they belong.
Hide your yellow asses
When you hear my song.
All over the jungle,
Up to old Haiphong,
Been crapping jelly petrol,
I been zap-zap-zap-zap Zapping the Cong.

Had a bomb in my 'copter
Called Linda B.
Saw a village and dropped her
On a mess of VC.
But I always say sorry
When I get it wrong.
Then I got to be zooming,
'Cause I'm Zapping the Cong.

Zapping the Cong
Back where they belong.
Hide your yellow asses
When you hear my song.
All over the jungle,
Up to old Haiphong,
Been crapping jelly petrol,
I been zap-zap-zap-zap Zapping the Cong.

I had a dream about going
With Ho Chi Minh.
But I'll only be crowing
When I'm zapping Pekin.
I'll be spreading my jelly
With a happy song
'Cause I'm screwing all Asia
When I'm zapping the Cong.

Zapping the Cong
Back where they belong.
Hide your yellow asses
When you hear my song.
All over the jungle,
Up to old Haiphong,
Been crapping jelly petrol,
I been zap-zap-zap-zap Zapping the Cong.

STIMULATING SONG

We know what we're doing.
We know what we're doing it for.
We know what we're doing.
We ought to know
For we've done it before.
We know what we're doing.
We know who we're doing it to.
We know what we're doing.
Out of the way
Or you know what we do.
Out of the way
Or we'll do it to you.

WHEN DREAMS COLLIDE

You're sucking your consensus when in walks the White
      Power Man
And he sells you a dream on the military instalment plan.
It's a supercharged vision and it shines like the Milky Way,
So you sign the agreement 'cause he says you'll never
      have to pay.

You're driving this Cadillac, your heart feels like the sun.
You're Rockefellersuperchrist, your numberplate just says
      One.
There's an engine full of gin and a blonde who works by
      steam
In your souped-up million-carat swinging hell of a dream.

Well the sunset looks like a Colour Supplement spread
And you can't slow down to count the Indonesian dead.
Then the brakes go crazy so you flash all your lights and
      pray
Because you've seen another dream and its travelling the
      other way.

It's a huge red tractor and it's coming on too damn fast
And the road's too narrow and you know that you'll never
      get past.
But the radio shouts that your dream has got to go
      through
And the last thing you see is the tractor-driver looks like
      you.

MOON OVER MINNESOTA

Mister Bondhus
Of Big Lake,
Minnesota
Made his mistake
When he raised ten sons,
Ten sons, ten sons,
To be Henry Fondas –
You know, the model of a democratic voter –
Didn't buy his sons guns.
Why?
Didn't want them to die
Or kill. Was that strange?
Well yes
I guess
But it makes for a change.
One day the draft board
Told Mister Bondhus
You can afford
To let the Army have a son
Just one
For a start,
You can part
With Barry, Barry,
Barry Barry Bondhus –
Your son.

Mister Bondhus
Of Big Lake,
Minnesota,
Downright
Forthright
Wouldn't send his quota.
Jefferson's sake
I'm not the kind of man who squanders
His seed.

I need
Barry, if you draft him
I've got nothing to
Look forward to
But ten coffins draped with the flag.
It became
A game
Of tag.
Will the draft board
Catch Barry Bondhus
To join the boys who died
On the side
Of the Lord
And the Big Lake
Minnesota
Draft Board?

Barry Bondhus
Of Big Lake,
Minnesota,
Ponders
As he wanders
Through the doors of the Draft Board
Office
Of his own accord.
Opens half a dozen files
Packed full,
Stacked full
With miles and miles,
Piles of government documents
About all the young men due to go far.
Then he lumps in,
Dumps in —
If I may quote a
Story from the Minneapolis Star —
Two full buckets of human excrement,
Stinking
Bondhus think-in

Excrement –
Nothing personal against the President –
It sounds as wild
As the action of a sewer –
realist child,
But the Draft Board files are all defiled.

Walt Whitman
Clarence Parker
Clarence Darrow
Ben Shahn.
Emma Goldman
Allen Ginsberg
Woody Guthrie
Tom Paine.
James Baldwin
Joseph Heller
Dr Benjamin Spock
Mark Twain

Yes all of the beautiful prophets of America
Write across the Minnesota sky:
Look look look at Barry Bondhus –
That boy can fly.

MAKE AND BREAK

Pass me the stethoscope of Albert Schweitzer,
Pall me the armoury of Mickey Spillane.
Put the mothers through the bacon-slicer,
Pick up the pieces and fit them together again.

Want to be humane, but we're only human.
Off with the old skin, on with the new.

We maim by night.
We heal by day.
just the same as you.

Fill all the area with whirling metal,
Five thousand razor-blades are slashing like rain.
Mr Hyde has a buddy called Jekyll
Picks up the pieces and fits them together again.

Want to be humane, but we're only human.
Off with the old skin, on with the new.
We maim by night.
We heal by day.
Just the same as you.

We treat the enemy like real blood brothers
God made the family a blessing and a pain.
Wives and husbands vivisect each other.
Pick up the pieces and fit them together again.

Want to be humane, but we're only human.
Off with the old skin, on with the new.
We maim by night.
We heal by day.
Just the same as you.

TO WHOM IT MAY CONCERN

I was run over by the truth one day.
Ever since the accident I've walked this way
            So stick my legs in plaster
            Tell me lies about Vietnam.

Heard the alarm clock screaming with pain,
Couldn't find myself so I went back to sleep again

So fill my ears with silver
Stick my legs in plaster
Tell me lies about Vietnam.

Every time I shut my eyes all I see is flames.
Made a marble phone book and I carved all the names
So coat my eyes with butter
Fill my ears with silver
Stick my legs in plaster
Tell me lies about Vietnam.

I smell something burning, hope it's just my brains.
They're only dropping peppermints and daisy-chains
So stuff my nose with garlic
Coat my eyes with butter
Fill my ears with silver
Stick my legs in plaster
Tell me lies about Vietnam.

Where were you at the time of the crime?
Down by the Cenotaph drinking slime
So chain my tongue with whisky
Stuff my nose with garlic
Coat my eyes with butter
Fill my ears with silver
Stick my legs in plaster
Tell me lies about Vietnam.

You put your bombers in, you put your conscience out,
You take the human being and you twist it all about
So scrub my skin with women
Chain my tongue with whisky
Stuff my nose with garlic
Coat my eyes with butter
Fill my ears with silver
Stick my legs in plaster
Tell me lies about Vietnam.

THE HOTPOT SAGA

In 1967 I became Granada fellow in the Arts at the University of Lancaster and moved north. It was one of the first resident writer jobs and nobody knew what I was supposed to do. I started a group called Song Workshop. We met once a week above a pub called the Shakespeare (Mitchell's Ales) and sang or read each other our latest poems and songs. But this began to seem ingrown and so we decided to write a show.

I produced a scenario. It was a kind of black panto about a race war between Yorkshire and Lancashire. It began with the return of young pop star Jack Hotpot to Lancaster, a Lancaster threatened by the evil giant of Yorkshire. Jack was accompanied by his pet flea, Enoch, but I'm getting ahead of myself. Each member of Song Workshop chose a scene to write. The conditions were that it must stick to the plot line, should include at least a couple of songs, but it could be written in any style. This became known as the Patchwork Theory of Structure. Put a dark square next to a light square etc – just as you do when constructing a poetry reading or a jazz concert.

A group of professional actors who were staging *Godot* at the University became involved, so that we found ourselves with Brian Murphy playing Widow Hotpot, a glorious Dame to end all Dames.

Towards the end of the writing period I saw Lon Chaney in *The Wolfman* on TV and became obsessed with its recurring couplet:

Even a man whose heart is pure, and says his
prayers at night
May turn into a wolf when the wolfbane blooms,
and the autumn moon is bright.

It changed the course of the show. Jack Hotpot suddenly
gained a secret identity as the Great Wolf of Lancashire,
preaching the gospel that all Lancastrians must become
werewolves in order to fight the Yorkshire Giant.

Members of the Workshop included the poet David
Craig, Greg Stephens, Boris and Maggie Howarth, all of
whom I was to work with again. At that time Boris was
fanatically into electronic music while Greg was a down-
to-earth folk singer and they had some noisy clashes. But
they soon learned to respect each other, and later, when
the Howarths joined John Fox and Sue Gill in Welfare
State International, they often called on Greg.

Two of the songs from the show, *Maximum Security Girl*
and *Ride The Nightmare* turned up again and again in
different shows because nothing else seemed to fit. This is
called re-cycling.

Composers: GREG STEPHENS and BORIS HOWARTH

Performed: Morecambe, 1968.

23

VICTORY MARCH SONG

We weathered the storm and we bore off the crown,
Won our spurs and gained the whiphand.
We quelled them and checked them, we trampled them
      down.
We'll live off the fat of the land.

They've gone to the dogs and they've bitten the dust –
Conquer, vanquish and overthrow.
They're routed, they're drubbed, they're upset and
      nonplussed,
We've licked, swamped and worsted the foe.

They burned all their boats and they scuttled their ship –
Bootless, sterile botchers and fools.
There's many a slip twixt the cup and the lip,
Flash in the pan between two stools.

LOVE DUET

I'm poor.
I'm broke.
But a skint bint
Can please a broke bloke.
we've got that much in common,
that's enough for me.

I'm dim.
I'm dum.
but a deadhead
Can love a crumbum.
We've got that much in common,
That's enough for me.

So I'm a maniac for marriage,
For I know that we'll pull through.
Yes we'll live in a derelict railway carriage
On Park Drive butts from the Municipal loo.

Well I can make it.
and I can make it.
If we can't make it
Well, we'll just fake it,
we've got that much in common,
that's enough for me.

I'm white.
I'm white.
so the Kiddie-winkies
Will be all right,
We've got that much in common,
That's enough for me.

So we're prepared to go the distance,
For in thirty years or more.
I'll have saved a pile on the National Assistance.
And I'll get a job in a surgical store.

We've got that much in common,
Plenty in common,
And that's enough, more than enough,
That's enough for me.

MAXIMUM SECURITY GIRL

Some girls are searching for marzipan visions
Some of them want nothing but eternal laughter
Some want a surgeon to make their decisions
But this girl knows what she's after –

She wants a town that has no people
So she's never in a crowd
She wants a town that has no people
Where strangers aren't allowed
She wants the countryside disinfected
So that stinging nettles won't grown
And a maximum security prison
For everyone she doesn't know

Then she'll be safe
That's what she said
Safer than insurance
Safer than the dead
She wants to be the safest person
In this dangerous dangerous world
Maximum security girl

She wants a house that has no windows
So the sun can't hurt her skin
She wants a house that has no windows
So the neighbours can't look in
She wants a maximum security garden
With land-mines planted in the ground
And a hundred and one alsatians
And electric fences all around

Then she'll have peace
That's what she said
Safer than insurance
Safer than the dead
She wants to be the safest person
In this dangerous dangerous world
Maximum security girl

CLOBBER A COPPER

In the blue and golden mornings of my childhood days
My father used to rock me on his knee
And he seemed so like a hero to my trusting gaze
And this was the advice he gave to me . . .

Clobber a copper for Christmas
That's what you have to do
Clobber a copper for Christmas
Don't take any sewage from the boys in blue.
If you're cuddling your fiance and a bogie should pass
And he hollers at you: "What all this then, keep off the
grass"
Just hit him with your handbag he's a traitor to his class
So clobber a copper today.

Do a detective for daddy
Blessings will fall on you
Do a detective for daddy
Don't take any sewage from the boys in blue.
If your handsome lodger offers you a stick of Blackpool rock
Then takes your hand so gently and says: "Will you mend
my frock?"
Just pick a rozzer random-like and boot him round the
block
Yes, do a detective today.

Slaughter a sergeant on Sunday
If you are feeling blue
Slaughter a sergeant on Sunday
Don't take any sewage from the boys in blue.
If Eamonn's on the telly and the budgie is sick,
If your son is down the boozer and your daughter's up the
stick
Just batter in a bobby with a half of a brick
Yes slaughter a sergeant
Do a detective

Clobber a copper
Rough up a rozzer
Batter a Bobby today . . .

RIDE THE NIGHTMARE

*I was zooming round the Universe feeling like Desperate
Dan
I was bombing them at random looking for Charlie Chan
I looked and saw a continent without a single man
Which they told me was Asia but it looked more like
Aberfan

So ride the nightmare
Jump upon its hairy back
Ride the nightmare
Ride until your mind goes black
It's the 21st century werewolf
21st century werewolf
21st century werewolf and it's coming this way

Well the charity lady wiped the diamonds from her eyes
and said
"I've been saving all my money but the African dead stay
dead
I'm sending them elastoplast and dunlopillo bread –
But they wrote me a letter saying: Send us guns instead"

So ride the nightmare
Jump upon its hairy back
Ride the nightmare
Ride until your mind goes black
It's the 21st century werewolf
21st century werewolf
21st century werewolf and it's coming this way

Well the rich white Englishman can easily ignore the rest
For the poor are just a bore and who can *use* the starving
and oppressed?
They're burning while you tell yourself there's nothing
you can do
When your turn comes they'll do just the same for you

So ride the nightmare
Jump upon its hairy back
Ride the nightmare
Ride until your mind goes black
It's the 21st century werewolf
21st century werewolf
21st century werewolf and it's coming this way . . .

*This first verse was rewritten around 1986 and it now goes –

I was zooming round the universe feeling like Sylvester
Stallone
I was bombing them at random looking for Gadaffi's home
I saw a Royal baby in a cradle of silver lace
And I saw another baby with flies feeding out of his
face . . .

MOVE OVER, JEHOVAH
or
THE MAN WHO SHOT EMILY BRONTE

Albert Hunt, who once staged the Russian Revolution in
Bradford, was approached by the National Association for
Mental Health to produce a theatre piece for a conference
of about 200 psychiatrists and psychiatric social workers in
Holland Park Comprehensive School.

Albert recruited me, John Fox from Leeds (who was on
the verge of forming Welfare State International), some of
my Song Workshop gang from Lancaster and a whole gang
of his students. After lots of discussions, Albert and I told
the NAMH that we wanted to stage the Bible. They were
very nice about it. So we started work.

It was another group-written show, based on stories
from the Bible, all related to madness. We saw Moses and
Aaron as two psychiatrists in charge of the Children of
Israel, mental patients who were not allowed to touch
each other, but who managed to get away with quite a lot
of touching, especially if Moses could be persuaded to go
mountain-climbing.

But up above was a platform from which the Earth was
watched, with beady eyes. Jehovah was an RAF Group
Captain, forever angered by the antics of humanity, ever
ready to press the 'Lice', 'Plague', 'Famine' or 'Boils'
buttons on his Smiter. Jesus was a gentle hippy, in sandals
of course, very sentimental but not at all anxious to go
down and be crucified. Satan was a beautiful secretary
biding her time, while the Holy Ghost was a hip character
in shades and an Italian suit, manipulating Jehovah and
Jesus with a view to taking over power. (This was one of

those shows which called, inevitably, for *21st Century Werewolf* – see *The Hotpot Saga*).

There were ructions within the group, mainly because Albert and I couldn't understand the wild writings of John Fox. John decided to concentrate on the programme, which turned out to be an extraordinary plastic bag for each delegate, containing all sorts of literature, some fairly scurrilous, plus samples of carpeting and anything else John could scrounge free. (Later John's writing became a lot clearer or I became more intelligent – anyway I love his writing now).

It was a long show but it had some wonderful moments. Some delegates loved it and some hated it. All I regret is that the camel we'd ordered which was to stand in the school playground as they left without any explanation was held up in traffic and never showed.

The *Lullaby to be sung by the mother of Moses* was written with the help of my daughter Sasha Mitchell, who was then about five.

Composer: BORIS HOWARTH

Performed: Holland Park Comprehensive School, 1968.

LULLABY TO BE SUNG BY THE MOTHER OF MOSES WHEN SHE LEAVES HIM IN THE BULRUSHES

There's nothing I can give you any more,
Except a quiet game for playing.
I took a gourd and dried it in the sun,
I hollowed it while you were sleeping.
I filled the gourd with silver desert sand
So you could make it whisper with your hand.
Now it makes a soft sound, a soft sound,
Nobody could hear except a baby.

THE VIOLENT GOD

Barbed wire all around the Garden of Eden
Adam was conscripted for the First World War
And it's still going on, and it's still going strong –
Hail to the violent god.

The old survivor said: I was in Belsen,
I'm grateful to god because he got me out of Belsen,
When I die please bury me in Belsen –
Hail to the violent god.

The god of hunger eats the people of India
The god of law and order spends most of his time
Smiling at the back of torture rooms –
Hail to the violent god.

Children were smitten with parents.
The black man was smitten with the white man.
The white man was smitten with the motor car –
Hail to the violent god.

Spastics teach us how to have pity
Leukaemia teaches us the dangers of anarchy
Schizophrenia teaches us sanity –
Hail to the violent god.

LASH ME TO THE MAST!

This was the follow-up to Lancaster Song Workshop's *The Hotpot Saga*. Greg Stephens suggested that we dramatize the *Odyssey*, and for a group which wrote by dividing a plot up into scenes and writing a scene each (with me as script editor, suggesting cuts and rewrites) it was ideal.

We decided to hire the Grand Theatre in Lancaster, where Sarah Bernhardt once played. Then we had a crisis. Boris and Maggie Howarth felt that we should look beyond the university audience. They suggested that admission to the show should be free. It was an ultimatum. We needed money to hire the theatre, but we needed Boris and Maggie even more. So we raised money by holding the University of Lancaster's first jumble sale and by a thrown-together rock concert.

The Grand Theatre is near some of Lancaster's slums, and when some of the local kids realised something was happening in the Grand, they moved in for rehearsals – for all the rehearsals. In a way, they took over. We discovered that they were bored by anything which went on too long, especially dialogue. And when they were bored they'd run up and down and muck about with the lights and even, in one case, pull knives on the cast. But they enjoyed songs, even the odd love song and they loved action.

My favourite scene, written under the Patchwork Theory of Structure – which permits each author to follow his or her own style – was the return of Ulysses to be greeted by his faithful hound, which in this case turned out to be a worm that encircled the stage and the proud possessor of 26 legs. This was the work of Boris Howarth, poet, performer, composer and clown.

I had great trouble with one of my two scenes, in which Ulysses tells Penelope that after his years away at war and wandering the Mediterranean, he has to go on a pilgrimage to purge himself. It didn't mean anything to the kids and in the end I produced this drastic rewrite:

Enter ULYSSES. He sees PENELOPE surrounded by suitors.

ULYSSES: (to audience) Look, I've been fighting in the Trojan War for ten years. And then I've been wandering all over the Mediterranean for ten years and all my men have been drowned or turned into pigs or eaten by monsters. And finally I get home and what do I find? A whole lot of blokes making up to my wife. What shall I do?

AUDIENCE: (invariably and without being led): Kill! Kill! Kill:

Blackout and noise of furious fighting.
Lights up on ULYSSES and PENELOPE on top of a heap of dead suitors.

CURTAIN.

Idelogically dodgy? Sure. But it worked.

Composers: BORIS HOWARTH and GREG STEPHENS.

Performed: Grand Theatre, Lancaster, 1969.

HUNGRY SONG

Anchovies in aspic
With marinated aubergines.
Beetroot bellies in brandy
With a bucket of Heinz Baked Beans.
Alligator puree and I don't care
If you serve it with bacon rind,
But gastronomic pornography
Is booting me out of my mind.

Caviar and cake mix
Makes coriander chocolate cheese.
Chutneyed carrots and coffee –
Won't you slice me a doorstep please?
Pass me down a mousse with its antlers on
You can cook it in Fairy Snow,
For gastronomic pornography
Is dragging me down so low.

Gammon stuffed with garlic,
Geraniums and gooseberry fool.
Grouse, gazpacho and ginger,
Burn your kitchen and leave to cool.
I want Mrs Beeton to be my man
And Elizabeth David too,
For gastronomic pornography
Makes my stomach feel like a zoo.

THE HAIRY MEN FROM THE HILLS

We are the Hairy Men from the Hills
We deal very hairily with anyone who gums us up
We are the Hairy Men from the hills
And that about sums us up
We are the Hairy, very very Hairy
Hairy Men from the Hills

CALYPSO'S SONG TO ULYSSES

My hands are tender feathers,
They can teach your body to soar.
My feet are two comedians
With jokes your flesh has never heard before.

So try to read the meaning
Of the blue veins under my skin
And feel my breasts like gentle wheels
Revolving from your thighs to your chin.

And listen to the rhythm
Of my heartbeat marking the pace
And see the visions sail across
The easy-riding waters of my face.

What is sweeter than the human body?
Two human bodies as they rise and fall.
What is sweeter than two loving bodies?
There is nothing sweeter at all.
Lose yourself, find yourself,
Lose yourself again
On the island of Calypso.

TAMBURLANE THE MAD HEN

Tamburlane is a play to be performed by primary school children and it deals with an anarchic rock 'n' roll hen who saves the people of London from a monster called Supercrab.

It was commissioned by Mike Kustow for a season of children's plays which somehow never happened but which led to the publication of the Methuen Young Drama *Playspace* volume in which the text and music can be found.

The play was written in twenty-four very happy hours. It leaves gaps which have to be filled by speeches written or improvised by the actors.

Composer: TONY ATTWOOD.

Performed: Many primary schools, 1970 onwards.

IT'S A SMASHING FEELING

It's a smashing feeling
On a Monday morning
The sting of the toothpaste
And the flavour of the flannel
And the sunshine cereal soggy in the plate

It's a smashing feeling
On a Monday morning
Your socks in the puddles
And the perfume on the buses
And the friendly underground, I can hardly wait

For that smashing feeling
On a Monday morning
The factory's music
And the gossip in the office
But there's one ingredient makes it all so great –

Work
There's nothing like a good hard slog
Work
Whether you're a clippie or a cop
Work
Don't waste any time in the bog
Work
Work work work work work work
Until your head goes pop.

TAMBURLANE ROCK

I'm a freaky kind of fowl
With bellbottom legs
I'm a sort of Mick Jagger
Laying oblong eggs.

Tamburlane . . . the Mad Hen
Tamburlane . . . the Mad Hen

Now I couldn't cluck or crow
To save my soul
But I'm a farmyard fanatic
For rock 'n' roll

Tamburlane . . . the Mad Hen
Tamburlane . . . the Mad Hen

I like to mess around
But I don't mean no harm
I'm a sort of dropout
From a battery farm

Tamburlane . . . the Mad Hen
Tamburlane . . . the Mad Hen

And if anybody asks you
Who sang this song
Tell them – Tamburlane the Mad Hen
Been here and gone

Tamburlane . . . the Mad Hen
Tamburlane . . . the Mad Hen

TYGER

"A celebration of the life and work of William Blake". It took years to write, mainly because of my fear of writing a full-length show. If a poetry reading flops, it's painful. But if a play is bad, you have the guilt of letting down a company.

Nagged by Ken Tynan, my friend, I eventually finished it in Yorkshire. He accepted it and slotted it into the National Theatre repertory while Sir Laurence Olivier was out of the country.

The main reason for writing the show was that I believe great speeches like *What is the Price of Experience* and great songs like *A Poison Tree* should be heard on the stage. (Blake used to sing his *Songs of Innocence and of Experience*.)

As composer I wanted the nearest I could find to a British Duke Ellington and, after listening to many records, decided on Mike Westbrook. It was the right choice. Not only is Mike Blake-like in many ways, but he has gone on to set many other Blake lyrics.

In the lyrics which follow, one, *A Man May Be Happy*, is taken directly from a letter which Blake wrote to the Reverend Trusler, an insensitive patron. I simply cut it up into lines and asked Mike Westbrook to set it and I include it simply as an example of that odd procedure.

In the other lyrics I stooge for Blake – Mrs Blake sings *The Children of Blake*, the Three Randy Women appear in response to Blake's sexual frustration, the *Quintet Song* is sung by Tennyson, Browning, Whitman, Edward Lear and Kipling. *Happy Birthday William Blake* is sung by a black

Lord Byron accompanied by Willy Wordsworth on drums, Percy Bysshe Shelley on bass guitar, Samuel Taylor Coleridge and John Keats. And they're joined by Allen Ginsberg, Shakespeare and other groovers. Most of this happens at a birthday party for Blake which ends in chaos and Mrs Blake saying: "At least the Bronte Sisters would have helped us clear up."

There were various attempts to tone down *Tyger*. The Lord Chamberlain had been abolished in 1968, which made possible the great flowering of fringe theatre in the Seventies and Eighties, but the fact that the play used the word clitoris caused walk-outs (led by husbands invariably) and led the management to put a notice in the foyer saying ". . . Tyger is perhaps not suitable for children". I objected but was overruled. The children who did come loved the show.

The plot followed the attempts of a good man to survive in a corrupt society and its targets included the rulers of the art world, monarchy, the Army and Mr Enoch Powell whose 1968 "Rivers of Blood" speech still has its deadly influence today. The show was furiously attacked by some critics and warmly defended by others. The result was that the cheap seats were filled and the expensive seats half-empty.

Looking back, Ken's initial idea of doing it in the Roundhouse, where we could have had huge Blake stained glass windows, would have made far more sense than performing in a conventional West End theatre where we weren't even allowed to put Blake pictures on the walls. But it was fun.

Composer: MIKE WESTBROOK.

Performed: National Theatre at the New Theatre, London, 1971, directed by Michael Blakemore and John Dexter.

Published: Jonathan Cape, 1971, LP, RCA, 1971.

A MAN MAY BE HAPPY

I feel that a man may be happy in This World.
And I know that This World
Is a World of imagination & Vision.
I see All I Paint In This World,
But Every body does not see alike.
To the eyes of a Miser a Guinea
Is more beautiful than the Sun,
& a bag worn with the use of Money
Has more beautiful proportions
Than a Vine filled with Grapes.
The tree which moves some to tears of joy
Is in the eyes of others
Only a green thing that stands in the way.

THE CHILDREN OF BLAKE

The children of Blake dance in their thousands
Over nursery meadows and through the sinister forests,
Beyond the spikes of cities, over the breasts of mountains,
The children of Blake dance in their thousands.
They dance beyond logic, they dance beyond science,
They are dancers, they are only dancers,
And every atom of their minds and hearts and their deep
        skins
And every atom of their bowels and genitals and
        imaginations
Dances to the music of William Blake.

RANDY WOMEN'S SONG

FIRST RANDY WOMAN
Dear Box Five Hundred and Five
I've got so much to give
My friends and enemies agree
I'm oversensitive.
The touch of a shadow
Puts my body in a shudder.
I can read in the dark with my thumb.
I'm so sexually aware
That a leather armchair
Makes me come and come and come.

SECOND RANDY WOMAN
Box Five-O-five, I'm a buxom widow.
I sleep on sheepskin with my arse out the window.
I need a bronco buster
To get his foot into my stirrup
'Cos I'm randy
Like brandy
And I flow like golden syrup.
Come on, bronco buster,
Get your foot in my stirrup.

THIRD RANDY WOMAN
Five-O-Five, I'm a sockaway rockaway wench.
I can make it on a tightrope or a corporation bench.
I'm not just one of your sexual freaks
But I've won prizes for the following techniques –
The Footsole Throbaway
The Rockinghorse Humjob,
The Olive Oil Helter-Skelter,
the Silverside Jump,
the Warm Swarm,
The Summertime Stoop
And the Velvet-lined Deep shelter.

I can take out your appendix without an incision.
I can make a half-arsed Andy Pandy come on like a Panzer
        Division.
If you can pass all these and a few other simple tests
I'll lullaby you by playing the Bells of St Mary's
With my breasts.

THREE RANDY WOMEN
Box five Hundred and Five
We know
You feel like a wooden cube
Box Five Hundred and Five
We could turn you
Into a golden globe
So you can roll
Let your soul roll
Let your soul roll
Roll away.

QUINTET SONG

We've come in an advisory capacity
To instruct you in the art of poesy
We live on Parnassus, it's a beautiful view,
Just follow in our footsteps and you'll join us too-oo-oo-oo

If you can

Skate on your toe-nails from here to the Aleutians
And be back in time for Armageddon.

If you can.

Run a dozen separate revolutions
And emerge with your beautiful head on.

If you can

Turn constipation
Into a song

If you can

Screw Euston Station
Till it chimes like a gong

And carve your verse on granite
With your luminous dong.

If you can do all this although you're feathered and tarred
If you can keep your arrows of desire hard
If you can live on biscuits and a union card

You'll be a man,
You'll be a world,
You'll be a planet,
You'll be a bard!

So sing it right
And get your cash on the night
And onward!
Upward!
You're bound to be famous.
Right on!
Avanti!
Venceremos!

For the poet is the man who runs a brothel at a loss.
He shares his Christmas pudding with Jesus on the cross.
If he kneels for a knighthood, just for a laugh
The Queen swings her sword back and chops him in half.

So sing it right
And get your cash on the night
Onward!
Upward!
Wise ignoramus
Right on!
Avanti!
And venceremos!
And happy birthday William Blake.

HAPPY BIRTHDAY WILLIAM BLAKE

When he was alive everybody used to put him down.
Now they're writing volumes and they say they're sad
       he's not around.
But they wouldn't know Blake if they saw him
And heard him
And shook him by the hand.
They wouldn't know Blake if they took him
And tried him
And shot him from the witness stand.

For Blake was a man like any other man
But he trained his hands to see
And he trained his tongue to pop out of his ears
And he cried with his toenails
And the hairs in his nostrils
Danced to the music of the oxygen.

And they took a thousand million bricks
And they laid down Blake like a foundation stone
And they built a city-prison on his chest
But nothing could hold him down.

For he took a draught of explosive air
And he shook off London like a crust.
And he sang as he stood on the edge of the world
And he worked as he stood as he sang
And he built Jerusalem
He built Jerusalem
With his soft hard
Hard soft hands.

So it's happy birthday William Blake
What you've done can never be undone.
Happy birthday William Blake
Tyger of Jerusalem and Lamb of London.
Happy birthday happy birthday
Happy birthday William Blake.

47

POETRY

Poetry
Glues your soul together
Poetry
Wears dynamite shoes
Poetry
Is the spittle on the mirror
Poetry
Wears nothing but the blues.

It's the mongoloid gargoyle that falls off the cathedral
To land on the crown of the Queen.
Grab it while you can, it's the magical needle.
It's bitter sixteen and its flesh is bright green.

Poetry
Glues you soul together
Poetry
Wears dynamite shoes
Poetry
Is the spittle on the mirror
Poetry
Wears nothing but the blues.

Nixon hasn't got it, but there's plenty in Fidel.
Slap your sherry trifle on my sewing-machine.
Bend it into bowlines but you'll never break it.
The only way to make it is the way you make it.
Only thing that matters is the way you shake it.

Poetry
Glues your soul together
Poetry
Wears dynamite shoes
Poetry
Is the spittle on the mirror
Poetry
Wears nothing but the blues.

MAN FRIDAY

Man Friday started life when Ann Scott commissioned it for the BBC's *Play For Today*. The attempt was to tell the Robinson Crusoe story from Man Friday's point of view. The story is told by Man Friday to his tribe and at the end the tribe makes a decision about whether to admit Crusoe.

My attempt was to step outside the white race and look at the criminal record of whites. My greatest pleasure was that my black friends and their children loved the play.

In order to write it I read a lot about tribal story telling. The most helpful book was Willard Trask's two-volume anthology, *The Unwritten Song*, which not only translates hundreds of tribal songs from all over the world but also describes ways in which songs are made.

Colin Blakely was the first Crusoe and Ram John Holder the first Friday in the TV version directed by the late James MacTaggart.

Halfway through writing it, I realised that the play could work on stage and soon the 7:84 Company toured it with Chris Asanti as Friday and Roger Sloman as Crusoe, plus Mike Westbrook's band, Solid Gold Cadillac.

Stage had the advantage that the audience could become members of the tribe and the decision as to whether or not to admit Crusoe could become a real debate with a real vote. Sometimes they voted to keep him, sometimes to throw him out.

Jack Gold directed a movie of it, which was made thanks to Peter O'Toole, who played Crusoe wonderfully. But the movie was much less successful than the TV or stage play.

Maybe my script was too wordy for the movies. And the fact that the producers cut Crusoe's suicide didn't help. It hadn't been there for kicks, it was in the nature of a prophecy about the future of the famous white race if it kept going the way it was going, Jack.

Finally the movie became a novel when I was told that unless I turned in a novelisation of the movie within ten days, somebody else would be given the task. I did it, and enjoyed it, and think the novel is good fun.

Composer: MIKE WESTBROOK

Performed: BBC TV, 1972. Stage, 7:84 Tour, 1973. Movie, 1975.

Published: 1974, Eyre Methuen.

FRIDAY BEGINS HIS STORY

As we have always been together,
Let us drink together.
As we are together now,
Let us dream together.
Let the wine flow,
Let my words flow
And I will try to tell my story truly,
As truly as I worship you,
My own people.

I am going to tell you about
A redfaced monster with a man inside its belly.
I am going to tell you about
A gabbling goat who could spit deadly thunder.
I am going to tell you about
The man who walks outside,
About the man who waits outside.

Close your eyes and see the story.
Close your eyes and see the story.

FRIDAY'S FOOTBALL SONG

Let me tell you of a war in which there was no fighting.
Let me tell you of a battle in which there was no hurting.
Victory did not matter at all, it did not matter,
And yet nothing mattered but the victory.
How you fought was the important thing
And yet how you fought was not important at all.
Let me tell you of the triumph of Friday
In the great war of football. . . .

FRIDAY'S SWIMMING SONG

Oh, swimming in the water
Is good, good, good.
Swimming in the water.
The water is a woman
So you plunge your body in
And then you draw it out again,
And then you plunge it a little deeper.
The water is a woman. . . .

MASTER AND FRIDAY

The sun can cook an island
But the moon cannot even boil an egg.

Nobody teaches the shark to swim
But the monkey never learns.

The wind can tear a forest down
But the tallest tree cannot harm the wind.

The body of Friday can show its happiness
But Master can only smile with half his mouth.

FRIDAY'S SONG OF LIGHT

Thank you, light.
Thank you, light.
I will always enjoy you
For that is all you ask.
I'm enjoying the light.
Let the whole world
Enjoy the light.
Let the sun and moon and stars
Enjoy their own light too.

THERE WAS A MAN

There was a man whose skin was covered with thorns.
There was a man whose skin was covered with thorns.
There was a man whose skin was covered with thorns.

May I take my knife and shave away your thorns?
May I take my knife and shave away your thorns,
So your skin may feel the fingers of the air?

No, no, I am disarmed without my thorns.
No, no, I am ashamed without my thorns.
No, no, for your knife hurts my thorns so badly.

There was a man whose skin was covered with thorns.
There was a man whose skin was covered with thorns.
There was a man —

THE TRIBE

The tribe changes
As a tree changes.

When the storm throws its weight against a tree
The tree bends away.
When the storm falls asleep upon the tree
The tree stands up again.

The tribe changes
As a tree changes.

The children are the blossoms of the tree,
They laugh along its branches.
The old are the fruit of the tree,
They fall when they are ready to fall.

The tribe changes
As a tree changes.

Nobody tells the tree how it should grow.
Nobody knows what shape it will assume.
The tree decides the angle of its branches.
The tree decides when it is ready to die.

MIND YOUR HEAD

Written originally for the Liverpool Everyman. It was set on a London number 24 bus. In the first act the bus ran from Hampstead Heath to Pimlico. In the second act it was hijacked and taken off to Wales.

The driver of the bus was upset because his father (another bus driver) had been run over by a black bus without a number. He suspected his uncle (a ticket inspector) of being responsible. His uncle had married his (the driver's) mother – who was also his (the driver's) conductress, a Welsh socialist conductress who insisted on charging bloody tories double fare. It was Hamlet with a bus and a lot more songs. And a happy ending, because, although the Inspector turned out to be Hitler in disguise, the driver ended up by marrying his mother.

The hit of the show turned out to be *Bad Friday*, which has featured in several subsequent shows. The original version had Edward Heath instead of Mrs T.

The Stone Ground Freak Song is composed entirely of headlines from *Oz* magazine, the pot-smoker's *Beano*.

Composer: TONY HAYNES (Liverpool)
 ANDY ROBERTS (London)

Performed: Everyman Theatre, Liverpool, 1973.
 Shaw Theatre, London, 1974.

Published: Eyre Methuen, 1974.

HEAVEN IS A HILL CALLED HAMPSTEAD

Heaven is a hill called Hampstead
And Hampstead is heaven on a hill.

There's the garden where Keats heard the nightingale.
There's a scruffy little pub where they still serve ale.
There's a marvellous choice of secondary schools –
Some for the rich and some for the fools.

Heaven is a hill called Hampstead
And Hampstead is heaven on a hill.

Twice a year on the Heath they hold a wonderful fair
You can see the working classes there.
Half a million for a cottage but nobody cares
In a street of socialist millionaires.

Heaven is a hill called Hampstead
And Hampstead is heaven on a hill.

Daddy's drinking champers on an ocean liner
On his way to study acupuncture in China.
Did you ever hear a German girl swear?
Mummy wrote a novel about the au pair.

Heaven is a hill called Hampstead
And Hampstead is heaven on a hill –

Yes we'll take our stand
In liberal land,
Home of the financially free,
In heaven, heaven,
Heavenly, heavenly,
Hampstead North West Three.

WASH YOUR HANDS

HUSBAND: My well-swept house is almost in the country
      You can see woodlands from the upstairs
        window
      On Saturday and Sunday there's a deck-chair
        on the patio
      And there I drink a can or two of lager.

WIFE: Oh wash your hands, my darling,
      Wash your hands, my darling,
      Wash your clever hands.

HUSBAND: With my arm across my eyelids, I sleep very
        soundly.
      My wife likes Chopin but I favour Mantovani.
      My little girl of five goes to ballet class on
        Wednesday.
      My little boy of seven collects toy vehicles.

WIFE: Oh wash your hands, my darling,
      Wash your hands, my darling,
      Wash your gentle hands.

HUSBAND: Every other weekend I take to my mother
      A cake from the kitchen or flowers from the
        garden.
      I always have a word and a wave for the
        neighbours
      As I go to do the work which I never mention.

WIFE: Oh wash your hands, my darling,
      Wash your hands, my darling,
      Wash your loving hands.

HUSBAND: Sometimes I sit and stare at nothing
      Sometimes I sit and smile at nothing
      Sometimes I sit and think of nothing
      My job is torturing men and women

My job is torturing men and women
My job is —

WIFE; Oh wash your hands, my darling,
    Wash your hands, my darling,
    Wash your shaking hands.

THE STONE-GROUND FREAK SONG

Smile if you had sex last night.
Hey, you know any place I can crash?
Would-be leaders shoot on sight
But first I've got to get my stash.

We'll turn the lower East Side
Into a woodland glade.
You know a man must make his move
Before his move is made
And every home should have one
Every home should have one.

Jessie was a Trotskyite —
Well, you are what you eat.
But summer's here and the time is right
For dancing in the street.

Do it again like a nation on heat.
Keef is the working man's drummer.
Jelly roll gum drops are good to eat.
The missionary position is a bummer
But every home should have one
Every home should have one.

Who did Jagger ever kill?
Dear Doctor Hippocrates

I need five dozen ampules
Of amyl nitrate please.

There's a shmuck in the tall dark hallway
Blinded by tear gas and Mace,
But whoring along the Hudson
We'll win the human race
And every home should have one,
Every home should have one.

We were dragged to the place of sacrifice
By Honeybunch Kaminsky.
I have seen the bird of paradise
She has spread her wings before me.

I yelled: I agree with your tactics,
But I don't know about your goal.
But she called the Church of Anthrax
And the merciless mayhem patrol
And every home should have one
Every home should have one.

When the mode of music changes
The walls of the city shake.
Fortify the over-forties –
They've arrested a birthday cake.

Mr Freedom has the big one
Down on the sewage farm.
Put a real Queen in the palace,
The Madonna of Napalm.
Every home should have one,
Every home should have one.

Search for your brothers and sisters.
Mind your head. Mind your head.
If they offer you insurance –
Strike them dead.

If you make a revolution
Make it for fun.

You're part of the problem or part of the solution —
Men it can be done!
And every home should have one,
Every home should have one,
Every home should have one.

NEVER STOPS

The good go to heaven and the bad to hell,
But it doesn't always work out so neat.
The hero's found hanging in his prison cell,
The villain dies of blondes in a penthouse suite.

Now I know there's a product called freedom,
You can buy it in most of the shops.
And I know that peace is science fiction,
But I also know the Revolution never stops.

Everyone pays in the end they say,
But I know one thing for sure:
The rich haven't even begun to pay
For all they've done to the poor.

Now I know there's a lady called Justice,
Cos I saw her boozing with the cops,
And I know the blind are killing the blind,
But I also know the Revolution never stops . . .

THE WORST THING

The worst thing in the world
The worst thing in the world
The worst thing in the world
Is what some people
Do to other people

Yes I know
The best thing in the world
The best thing in the world
The best thing in the world
Is what some people
Do for other people

But
The worst thing in the world
The worst thing in the world
The worst thing in the world
Is what some people
Do to other people.

BAD FRIDAY

SOLDIER   I was working for a farmer
But I answered him back
Got my wages on the Friday,
Plus the sack.
When I talked about the Union,
Farmer said to me:

FARMER   Don't you know what day
This happens to be?
It's Fuck Off Friday

That's the day I love.
When all of the losers
Get the shove.
I call it my day,
I can't wait till when
Fuck Off Friday
Rolls round again.

SOLDIER   Used to do a bit of dancing,
                 Rock 'n' roll.
                 My fiancee chucked me
                 'Cos I was on the dole.
                 Went down for a hand-out
                 To the DHSS
                 But the woman at the counter said:

CLERK   You're a mess –
                 It's Fuck Off Friday,
                 That's the day I love.
                 When all of the losers
                 Get the shove.
                 I call it my day,
                 I can't wait till when
                 Fuck Off Friday
                 Rolls round again.

SOLDIER   So I joined the Army
                 For the regular pay.
                 At least the British Army
                 Never turns you away.
                 I was walking through Derry,
                 Got shot in the head.
                 And as I lay dying
                 An angel said:

ANGEL   It's Fuck Off Friday,
                 That's the day I love.
                 When all of the losers
                 Get the shove.
                 I call it my day,

                        I can't wait till when
                        Fuck Off Friday
                        Rolls round again.

SOLDIER   Well the British Army
                        Bought my coffin for me
                        And my mother got a cable
                        From Mrs T.
                        But when she read her
                        Condolence note,
                        She sent her back a letter –
                        Here's what she wrote:

MOTHER   It's Fuck Off Friday,
                        That's the day I love.
                        When all the Tories
                        Get the shove.
                        I call it my day,
                        I can't wait till when
                        Fuck Off Friday
                        Comes to Number Ten.

COMPANY   Saturday . . . Sunday . . . Monday . . .
                        Tuesday . . . Wednesday . . . Thursday . . .

                        Fuck Off Friday
                        That's the day I love.
                        When all of the bosses
                        Get the shove.
                        I call it my day,
                        I can't wait till when
                        Fuck Off Friday
                        Comes to Number Ten.

MARIE LLOYD

Marie Lloyd was warm as kettles
And frank as celluloid
And her words could sting like nettles
Or caress like Marie Lloyd

> Marie Lloyd comes back and warm us
> Marie Lloyd return to us
> For your heart was as enormous
> As a double-decker bus

She had eyes like Dylan Thomas
And the wit of Nye Bevan
Marie Lloyd was taken from us
Send her back to succour man

> Marie Lloyd come back and warm us
> Marie Lloyd return to us
> For your heart was as enormous
> As a double-decker bus

Like a farted interruption
Of a speech by Sigmund Freud
Like Mount Etna in eruption
Is the heart of Marie Lloyd

> Marie Lloyd come back and warm us
> Marie Lloyd return to us
> For your heart is as enormous
> As a double decker bus

THE BUM-COLLECTOR'S SONG

Here I comes
With me bucket of bums
Isn't it a lovely day?

I live in the slums
With a posh set of drums
That I never have time to play

I've got double-jointed thumbs
And receding gums
But otherwise I'm OK

And when I meet my chums
Walking out with their mums
this is what I always say –

Here I comes
With me bucket of bums
Isn't it a lovely day?

MARRY YOUR MOTHER

M – A – Double R – Y
Your M–O–T–H–E–R.
Don't be shy
My litte laddie,
She was good enough for Daddy.
Boom! Boom!
Back to the womb!
Where'd you get that Mum from?
Marry your Mother today
And go back where you come from!

KARDIFF RULES, OK?

Between 1974 and 1975 I was Resident Writer at the
Sherman Theatre in Cardiff. I was promised the main
auditorium for a group-written show, complete with a
professional director and free admission for three nights.
All I had to do was to find that group.

It was a University post, but I found that almost all the
students were far too busy for my project – or maybe I
explained it badly. Finally I came across a bunch of people
at the local community bookshop – the 108 Bookshop.
They were all active in different causes – the Gypsy Action
Group, Housing Group, Women's Action Group etc. I
proposed that we write a show about these causes and
perform it ourselves. Led by the Women's Action Group
enthusiasm grew.

I invented a story framework for the show. A group of
delegates had been called together. They were the people
responsible for keeping the poor in slums, persecuting
gypsies, denying battered wives protection etc. But they
were forced to act out their *failures* in these fields – that is
the victories of the people. In this way, by celebrating the
small triumphs of the weak over the strong, we hoped to
present an evening of hope and struggle rather than
despair. I also encouraged everyone to use humour and
songs as weapons, rather than self-pity.

Late in the day we were joined by the Campaign for
Homosexual Equality and their section of the show was
one of the strongest. The CHE ballad here was interspersed
between acted scenes based on the experience of our

actors in Cardiff. On the first night, when a young actor in a spotlight sang "I am a homosexual" there was a rugged laugh from a few seats. But he waited till the laugh died and continued, aiming at the laughers, "And part of the human race", and his courage won the entire audience.

Mostly people wrote their own songs, but I contributed when asked (including a parody of Zipp-a-dee-do-dah called *Glad to be Gay*).

Our writing group called itself "Group Five – Total Insecurity" after the Group Four – Total Security men who patrolled the Sherman. The plot of our show involved the increasing presence of more and more heavily armed security persons. It also involved the worship of an octopus which spouted shaving foam from its tentacles. There was also a scene in which the entire cast donned Margaret Thatcher masks and sang *Try to be more like Margaret Thatcher to look at.* Since this was early 1975 it was a bit prophetic, though marred by the fact that we all made our own masks in a hurry and very few of them looked anything like Mrs T.

Composer: GEOFF PEARSON

Performed: Sherman Theatre, Cardiff, 1975.

CHE BALLAD

I'd like to tell a story
A story that is true.
If you'll kindly listen to it
You might see my point of view.
I am a homosexual
And part of the human race
But I hung my head
Hid my face

I went to school in Cardiff
Where I was taught to fear
The laughter all around me
When the teacher used a word like 'queer'
Now I'm grown up and I stay at home
Though my home's a dismal place
I just hang my head
Hide my face.

We've played that scene twice weekly
But now it's gone too far
So I'll go out and have a drink
In the pub they call Park Lane Bar.
I'll have a pint of bitter please.
But I've hardly had a taste
When I hang my head
Hide my face.

Well I'd like to go to Robert's Bar
Cos I've heard from some who've been
But I am much too nervous
For fear of being seen
So I'll go down to Mill Lane
That's another meeting place
If you hang your head
And hide your face.

My life is getting worse and worse
Too scared to make a friend
There's no one I dare look at
And I wish my life would end.
So I'll go and see my doctor
And I'll tell him my disgrace
And then I'll hang my head
And hide my face.

So much for Doctor Frankenstein.
What did his treatment do?
It's made me much more terrified
And it filled my nightmares too.
I am heading straight for suicide
I'm told that's commonplace.
Shall I hang myself
And hide my face?

But look – there is a poster
For the Cardiff branch of CHE
It says that homosexuals
Should be glad that they are gay.
So now I'm in the open
Though the open's a tough place
I don't hang my head
Or hide my face.

SCHOOLROOM SONG

There's all sorts of lovely
Clothes and toys
Some for girls
And some for boys

Billy has a stun gun
Susan has a dolly
Jimmy has a railway train
Jilly has a golly

Joan is frilly
She looks so cute
Freddy acts tough
In his cowboy suit

A Barbie doll
For pretty little Lily
And Action Man
For brave young Willy

But why does Billy get the gun
While Susan gets the dolly
Why does Jimmy get the train
While Jilly gets the golly

It's very logical indeed
The reason, dear, is this
A boy has got a penis
And a girl has a clitoris

BOOGIE TO BITS

Let your body hang loose
Now save your juice
Let a foot go tap
Slap . . . Slap
Now you getting the feel
Soon we do it for real
Begin to move
In a rockin groove
Now wait till the music hits

And then Boogie
Boogie to Bits

Put your hand on your hip
Let your backbone slip
Let your pelvis slide
Yes it's going for a ride
Don't matter how you look
Just let it cook
Add a little bit of jerk
Now we gettin down to work
Now wait till the music hits
And then Boogie
Boogie to Bits

You gotta flutter your hands
Wake up your glands
Get your ass in the scene
You know what I mean
Feel the beat through the floor
Feel the beat a little more
Hang out everything you got
Ready, ready to rock –
And wait till the music hits
And then Boogie
Boogie to Bits

TRY TO BE MORE LIKE MARGARET THATCHER TO LOOK AT

Try to be more like Margaret Thatcher to look at
Try to be more like Margaret Thatcher in every way
Try to be more like Margaret Thatcher to look at
Cos it's a Margaret Thatcher world – so hey, hey, hey!

THE FINE ART OF BUBBLE-BLOWING

Once upon a time there was a TV series called *Churchill's People*. Not many people watched it, partly because it started with Druids. There is something about Druids which makes an evening ten-pin bowling with Alan Whicker seem attractive. Many people disliked being categorised as Churchill's – personally I'd rather be one of Blake's blokes.

I wrote two of the plays. They were shown late in the series, when viewers had dwindled, but I was pleased with them mostly and the critics, notably the late great Gwyn Thomas, liked them.

In the first – *Silver Giant, Wooden Dwarf* – I'd been asked to deal with Runnymede, so I wrote a sad little comedy about King John's Saxon bathman (Dinsdale Landen) and his friendship with the Norman clerk who has to write out Magna Carta overnight (Patrick Troughton). Blondel had a part in it too, but there were no songs worth preserving.

The second – *The Fine Art of Bubble-Blowing* – was a sort of South Sea Bubble with pence instead of guineas, the story of a Scots mathematical genius (Tom Conti) who became the brains behind an East End gang (Arthur Mullard, Rita Webb and their ilk) who set up their own Stock Exchange. The following songs were sung straight to camera by the hero, who ended up with a government job.

Composer: STANLEY MYERS

Performed: BBC TV, 1975.

WHEN ONE DOG MEETS ANOTHER

When one dog meets another
They take time making friends.
They circle round each other
And sniff each other's ends.
But when man meets a stranger
He never can tell
If the scent of the other is danger –
For man, though he stinks, has no sense of smell . . .

SOUTH SEA BUBBLE SONG

From all those folk
Who do not have
It shall be grabbed away.
But those who have
Are granted more –
That's what the Gospels say.

But I would add
What I believe,
Though I have never read it:
To those who only
Seem to have
Is granted endless credit.

MY THREE SONS

I have three sons
And fine young sons
And which do you say does best, Sir?
One is a soldier
And one is a pimp
And the third a bold investor.

There's loot for the soldier
And whores for the pimp
Before their bodies fester –
But there's minus nothing
At ten per cent
For the damn-fool bold investor.

THE EIGHTEENTH CENTURY CON-MAN'S
APOLOGY TO THE TWENTIETH CENTURY

By all of those rules I could mention
The noose should have ended my plan,
But now I've an income and pension
For I am a government man.

For you it is hard to envision
A liar employed by the State,
Unless you make ample provision
For your relative distance in date.

Your statesmen don't base a career, Sir,
On profits from fraudulent crime.
But yours is the Honesty Era –
Corruption was rife in *my* time.

TOTAL DISASTER

In 1975 BBC TV had a bright idea. Three writers would meet for the first time on Monday. They'd thrash out an idea with a director and write a half hour play which would be cast, rehearsed and designed in time for transmission, live on Saturday night in a slot called *Eleventh Hour*.

John Bowen, Brian Clark and I met director Piers Haggard on the Monday. We talked about the events of the week which might give us a lead in our search for a plot. Next morning I was the only one of the three writers to come in with a plot outline, about a very timid man who's afraid of everything, goes on a cruise on an ultra-safe liner and ends up – after enduring every disaster in the book, on a desert island.

It wasn't *The Three Sisters*, but it was better than no story and most people grasped at it. John felt it wasn't at all the kind of play he wanted to be part of, so he left, leaving me and Brian to divide up the story. Which we did.

It turned, towards the end, into a roughneck parody of a Disaster Movie – with a chorus that went –

> You shook me like a disaster movie
> You shook me like a disaster movie
> You shook me like a disaster movie
> What a shame what a shame
> Gonna drown in my own flame.

When it came to title time I had my way. I said we should call it *Total Disaster* so that the *Daily Telegraph* critic would be able to say: ". . . er um this play was aptly named

Total Disaster, ha ha" which is exactly what he did.

Composer: ANDY ROBERTS

Performed: BBC TV 1975.

LULLABY TO BE SUNG BY SECURITY OFFICERS

The padlock's on the gateway of creation
The nightingale's been charged with getting high
The night-clouds all assemble like Alsatians
To howl this safety-conscious lullaby

The stars have put on their protective helmets
The sun has set in his red rubber gloves
The curtains of the sky close on their pelmets
What a wonderful setting for super-safety love

> Top security moon
> Great big yellow blob
> Top security moon
> Simply doing its job . . .

OCEAN LINER GOOD ADVICE SONG

To make good love on a ship
You don't have to be
A physical jerk –
Just mesh your flesh
Let your backbone slip
And let the motion
Of the ocean
Do all of the beautiful work

FINAL FINALE

Arrivederci, Western Civilisation!
You know you're headin'
For Armageddon,
Soon be forgotten.

Arrivederci, Western Civilisation!
I'd kiss you goodbye
But I'm scared that I
Might catch something rotten . . .

THE FREE MUD FAIR

From time to time I work at Dartington College of Arts in Devon. I go there to work with theatre students. My first projects there were massive – it was as if I thought that I'd never be able to come back, so everything had to be packed in, or as if I had to impress the hell out of the college by producing an enormous group-written show in record time. I asked too much of the students and even more of myself. Later I learned to take things a little easier.

My first project there was *Mass Media Mash* in 1974. We took one day as treated by the magazines, newspapers, TV etc, and we tried to dramatise the stories which interested us most. The structure was based on a rich newspaper proprietor and a woman who sold papers going through their day. My main contribution was a dramatisation of an interview with a Royal Marine in a Marine recruiting ad. The marine said: "I took to the Royal Marines like a duck to water". This became a recurring song in the Marine section: "Like a duck to water/Like a duck to water/I took to the Royal Marines/Like a duck to water". Later in the show it changed into: "Like a lamb to slaughter/Like a lamb to slaughter/I was led through Medialand/Like a lamb to slaughter." The whole show was a kind of revue.

My next project was the infamous eight hour *Mud Fair* on Vere Island in the middle of Totnes, which we renamed the Island of Angels. The idea was to do a show outside the college which could be enjoyed by kids. We wanted an all day show made up of sideshows and plays and operas and games, things happening simultaneously but no money. It was December, a very cold day. We spent the night before on the island with some braziers so we could guard all our instruments and tents. The show itself included a procession, two brief operas, a mock beauty contest, some Dennis the Menace plays, an escapologist, the Jumblies in a boat, free hot refreshments, fortune-telling, a speech of great pomposity, many brief plays both tragic and comic, fireworks and a dance of ghosts.

Composer: WILLIAM YORK.

Performed: The Island of Angels, Totnes, Devon, 1976.

GARDENING

EVE: At the heart of the Garden of Eden
                  Lay a pool of golden mud

                  I was the pool
                  And my name was Eve

                  One day I stood up like a fountain
                  And began to mould my body
                  Till it felt right and good

                  Then I made Adam out of the same golden
                  mud
                  I made him different for fun

ADAM: Thank you for creating me

EVE: Shall we make more people out of mud?

ADAM: Yes
                  You make some like me
                  I'll make some like you

EVE: Let's make them all different

ADAM: Why make them different?

EVE: For fun for fun
                  For fun for fun

ADAM: No . . . No . . .
                  Two kinds is enough
                  Two kinds is plenty

EVE (to audience):   My secret name is Peace
      (to ADAM)   All right, Adam

EVE and ADAM: So we made children out of the mud
                  Thousands of children out of the mud
                  Two kinds of children
                  Only two kinds
                  All of them totally different

A SEVENTH MAN

This was my adaptation of John Berger's fine study of migrant workers in Europe. It was built out of Berger's words and Mohr's photographs and out of rehearsals with the Foco Novo company.

In many ways it was the hardest adaptation job I ever attempted. The book was so complete as a work of art and I respected its creators so much that it was hard to take the kind of liberties you have to take in order to make a book work on the stage.

One of the pleasures of the production was working with Ralph Steadman, who designed the sets. Ralph introduced me to his theory of playwriting: "A show should be like a fairground. No ride should last longer than three minutes". It often seems true and useful when writing for jumpy, TV-tempo modern audiences.

Composer: DAVE BROWN.

Performed: Foco Novo tour and Hampstead Theatre, 1976.

THE MOTHER'S SONG

And he will go
Like all our strongest children
Yes he will go
He will be taken

Aiii Aiii

They'll take his body
I built it with my blood and milk
They'll take the courage
I taught him when I lay in labour

Aiii Aiii

They'll take his passion
They'll take his dreams
They'll take his hoping
They'll take his brains

Aiii Aiii

Yes he will go
Like all our strongest children
Yes he will go
He will be taken

Everything it taken
Everything is taken from us
Everything is STOLEN!

PEASANT SONG

The world
Is an arse
Made of stone
and the houses are arseholes

We eat
What we need
When we can
And our table's a coffin

Our sleep
Is a hole
In the night
Between twilight and milking

The churn
Fills with milk
Twice a day
And the milk churns are emptied

We're poured
On the fields
Twice a day
You can see the steam rising

The scalp
Of the earth
Must be combed
Both in autumn and famine

The bones
Of the earth
Metal bones
Must be dug by our fingers

It's time
Says the clock
On the church
For today's crucifixion

The world
Is an arse
Made of stone
And the houses are arseholes
Everything is taken
Everything is taken from us
Everything is taken

THE WEIGHING MACHINE

You buy a weighing machine
The kind made for a bathroom
With rubber on the platform
For bare wet feet.

You wrap it up in paper
You hurry through the city
Until you reach the station
And choose your street

And you sit there on the pavement
With your weighing machine unwrapped and displayed.
And you cry out, you cry out, all day long:
Your weight! Your true weight!
Your weight! Your true weight!

A whole day crying:
Your weight! Your true weight!

By the end of the day
You might have the cash
To pay for a meal
For one.

A whole day crying:
Your weight! Your true weight!

FACTORY SONG

Stamping, boring, pressing, beating,
The scream of hydraulic tools.
The shock of substance hitting substance
And one substance grating on another substance.
It takes a long time to get used to the noise.
The noise itself hits and grates.
Within the reverberations
There are insistent rhythms.
So every echo is interrupted.
Nothing begins and nothing fades away.

If noise slackens
Or if you leave the workshop,
The same insistent rhythms
Keep beating in your head.
You feel them,
Although you hear nothing –
It is like going deaf.

Silence here is deafness.

BUS STATION

Small town bus station
Mud and grass parking space
A mess of wooden huts

Small town bus station
In the air a cloud of sound
As journeys are explained

> There's always a wind in such places
> Grit and litter whirling around your feet
> You don't always cringe from the cold in such
> places –
> Sometimes you're flattened by the heat

Small town bus station
Migrants, soldiers, families
Who have to travel on

Small town bus station
The only thing you never see
Is anyone who's rich

MEDICAL

The fit are being sorted out from the unfit.
One in five will fail.
Those who pass will enter a new life.
One in five will fail.

SONG ABOUT MIGRANT WORKERS

They are not born.
They are not raised.
They are not schooled.
They do not vote.
They do not mate.
They do not strike.
They do not age.
They do not die.

They have a single function:
They work.

THE GOLD

To those who have machines,
Men shall be given.

To those with no machines,
Men shall be taken away.

The gold fell from very high in the sky.
So when it hit the earth
It went down very deep.

DAY OFF

Day off
Day off
What can you do with a day off
When you're saving up your money
Saving up yourself
When you're six months away from home

> You wash your clothes
> You write to your family
> Play cards or wank or weep
> You shave your face
> Shave it again
> Or do something active like get in some sleep

Time off
Time off
What can you do with time off
Except pass the time
Except pass the time
Except kill the time
that's killing you

THE WORKERS

They build your skyscrapers
Lay your motorways
Make your castings
Clean your cities
Man your assembly lines
Quarry your minerals
Load your lorries
Bury your pipelines
How do they live?
Treated like shit.

We don't ask your pity
For those who plough the fields of stone
Or for the men in narrow-eyed cities
Struggling to endure alone.
Workers don't need our fine feelings
They've got feelings of their own inside them.
All that they demand from us
Is that we should fight beside them.

ROUND THE WORLD IN EIGHTY DAYS

I've always been a Jules Verne fan. When Geoffrey Reeves asked me to write lyrics for the Nottingham Playhouse adaptation of *Round the World In Eighty Days* I had to do it. As usual there was very little time, so composer Bill Scott came to stay and he wrote tunes in one room while I wrote about four or five lyrics a day next door.

Nearly all our songs were used, barring one marathon number which listed the title of almost every book M. Verne ever wrote. But I was allowed to write the show's publicity button, which read *Jules Rules*.

I enjoyed the show greatly but it's never been revived. Despite that, *Judy's Song* has been used in various shows since. At the last moment I was asked to write a song for the actress Judy Riley to sing while scrubbing the deck of an ocean liner. I wrote the lyric while waiting for an AA man to rescue our broken-down car outside Nottingham and phoned it through to Bill. Next day Judy was rehearsing it.

Many of the lyrics come straight out of Verne's visions – his phrase about "the happy-go-lucky miners of San Francisco" sparked off one, while another celebrates the Japanese acrobatic troupe he named *The Long Noses*. *The Song of the Stokers* was later used in Welfare State International's *Raising the Titanic*.

Composer: BILL SCOTT.

Performed: Nottingham Playhouse, 1977.

WHAT HE'S NOT

Mister Phileas Fogg
In 1872
Was the occupant of
The house where Sheridan died.
Mister Phileas Fogg
Was nothing like me and you.
Byron's exterior
Was far inferior
But no-one had ever seen Mister Fogg's inside.

We know almost nothing about him
And we want to know the lot
So we'll try to define Mister Phileas Fogg
In terms of what he's not.

He's not a
Lawyer or a broker
Or a farmer or a joker
Or a wicked boss who makes his workers slog.
He's not a
Merchant or a tailor
Or a soldier or a sailor
We can only be sure that he's Phileas Fogg.

He's not a
Miser or a spender
Not too tough and not too tender
Well he wouldn't risk his life to save a frog.
He doesn't
Lecher, bet or guzzle,
He's a fascinating puzzle
But the evidence shows that he's Phileas Fogg.

He doesn't
Join great institutions
Or engage in revolutions
He's so enigmatic that the world's agog.

Of his club
We can inform you
He's applied to join the Reform, who
Unanimously elected Phileas Fogg.

Mister Phileas Fogg
In 1872
Was the occupant of
The house where Sheridan died.
Mister Phileas Fogg
Was nothing like me and you.
Byron's exterior
Was far inferior
But no-one had ever seen Mister Fogg's inside.

THE REFORM CLUB

The Reform Club The Reform Club
Someone's been readin' my Times.
What's in the Telegraph, Chumley?
Several unspeakable crimes.

The Reform Club The Reform Club
How will old Benson recoup?
Five over par at Saint Andrews.
Waiter, there's blood in my soup!

The Reform Club The Reform Club
He's not insane if he hunts.
Young Booley's just back from Injah.
You went to Cambridge sir?
                                    Once.

The Reform Club The Reform Club
We were both in the same dorm.
He went and married a Grierson.
I sleep here. At the Reform.

The Reform Club The Reform Club
At least *my* tenants get fed.
I think this armchair's got dandruff.
How will we know when we're dead?

DREAM TRAVEL

Dream travel
Minutes and hours and days
Dream travel
Wrestling with jungles
Or floating on the haze
Dream travel
Time is the name of the stream
Tell me when I am
And where's my name
For the whole world seems a dream

I saw
A waterfall climbing a pyramid
The Vikings in St Peter's Square
A crystal grotto full of leopards
The Statue of Liberty
With cobras in her hair

I saw
The cannibal dancers of Moscow
And a Taj Mahal that worked by steam
I saw the ostriches flying over Amsterdam
Travelling in a dream

Dream travel
Minutes and hours and days
Dream travel
Wrestling with jungles
Or floating on the haze
Dream travel
Time is the name of the stream
Tell me when I am
And where's my name
For the whole world seems a dream

I saw
A Syrian iceberg exploding
And a submarine with ten left feet
A cloud which was driven by clockwork
And a mountain of blubber
Up in Downing Street

I saw the Mardi Gras of the Walrus
And heard the belly of India scream
And the Sphinx of Fujiyama called my name
Travelling in a dream

Dream travel
Minutes and hours and days
Dream travel
Wrestling with jungles
Or floating on the haze
Dream travel
Time is the name of the stream
Tell me when I am
And where's my name
For the whole world seems a dream

THE SONG OF THE STOKERS

jesus but its hard   feeding that furnace
jesus but its hard   heaving that coal
jesus but its hard   feeding that furnace
jesus but its hard   and it shrivels your soul

it's just like

working in a quarry on the surface of the sun   agh hu
working in a quarry on the surface of the sun   agh hu
dig ten tons of the heavyweight golden
watch who you're splashing with that load of molten
working in a quarry on the surface of the sun   agh hu

takes a hundred thousand shovelfuls of lava to fill that
truck
        jesus but its hard   working in the quarry
i shovelled bout a million but it looks like it never fills up
        jesus but its hard   working on the sun
they say it sprung a leak and they say I got to double my
speed
jam that shovel in and heave another heap of heat

jesus but its hard   baking my brains now
jesus but its hard   baking my feet
jesus but its hard   baking my heart now
jesus but its hard   and i'm hard baked meat.

ELEPHANT SONG

I trapped an elephant
Mated that elephant
I bred this elephant
I trained my elephant
I ride my elephant
I keep my elephant

This is my elephant

You have money
Your friends have money
Your women have money
Your clerks have money
Your soldiers have money
Your queen has money

I have my elephant

       We have enough to eat
       We ask no more
       A man who has no elephant
       Is truly poor

Go trap your money
Go mate your money
Go breed your money
Go train your money
Go ride your money
And keep your money

I'll keep my elephant

ENGLISH LOVERS

English
Lovers
Are somewhat under-rated
English
Loving
Is always understated
We don't touch much
We leave that to the Poles and Dutch
For
English
Lovers
Don't yearn
To be terrific
English
Loving
Is most unscientific
So give me your hand
I'll never ask for more
For English
Lovers
Are supreme
Because they're
English
English to the stiff upper core.

POPPY JUICE

Oh oh poppy
oh oh pop
oh oh poppy juice
oh oh poppy

Poppy juice
I'm flying
poppy juice
stopped trying
poppy juice poppy juice
You help me see the joke.
Poppy juice
I'm falling
Poppy juice
I'm calling
Poppy juice poppy juice
I'm going down in smoke.

Wand'ring through a forest
Stroking every tree
A choir of leaves begins to sing
Then I'm in a woman
Underneath the sea
Everybody wants me to be king

Oh oh poppy
oh oh pop
oh oh poppy juice
oh oh poppy

I catch a double-decker
Painted like a bull
I giggle as the bus begins to rain
Suddenly I'm falling –
Take another pull . . . mmmmm
Slow motion surfing – feeling no pain

oh poppy juice
I'm flying
poppy juice
stopped trying
poppy juice poppy juice
You help me see the joke.
Poppy juice
I'm falling
Poppy juice
I'm calling
Poppy juice poppy juice
I'm going down in smoke . . .

CHINESE TYPHOON

The mercury's rising and falling
The barometer's lost its head
The ocean's rising in surges
And the sun has drowned in a mist of red

Reef down the sails!
Stash away the pole-masts!
All hands forward to the bow!
Set a single triangular sail!
Hang on tight! She's coming now!

Typhoon! Typhoon!
Four times faster than a record-breaking train!
Typhoon! Typhoon!
Mountains of water and whips of rain!
The violent ocean shakes and knocks
With boat-crushing shocks and counter-shocks
For this is the winter equinox
And you wouldn't even notice if we hit the rocks
Typhoon! Chinese typhoon!

Suddenly the typhoon's over.
There are smiles in the saloon
As the passengers rehearse their stories
For the families they're joining soon.
"Did you have a nice trip?" "Satisfactory,
Apart from a Chinese typhoon."

HOTEL VERANDAH

FOGG AND AOUDA
This is a casual breakfast
On a hotel verandah
With a breathtaking harbour view
Just a casual breakfast
On a hotel verandah
With a casual remark or two

FOGG
May I pass you
The toast and tea?

AOUDA
The Chinese are terrible
At kedgeree.

FOGG AND AOUDA
This is a casual breakfast
On a hotel verandah
With a breathtaking harbour view
Just a casual breakfast
On a hotel verandah
With a casual regret or two

AOUDA
Do you like me?

FOGG
Absolutely

AOUDA
Will you miss me?

FOGG
Acutely

AOUDA (aside)
I may have feelings
And those feelings may weep
They're inaudible even to me.

FOGG (aside)
I may have feelings
but they're buried so deep
That nobody ever will see

FOGG AND AOUDA
This is a casual breakfast
On a hotel verandah
With a breathtaking harbour view
Just a casual breakfast
On a hotel verandah
With a breathtaking view of you.

THE LONG NOSES

We are
The Japanese Acrobatic Troup
Of the Honourable William Batulcar
This is
Our last performance before our departure
For the US of Americar
We're the Long Noses
The Long Noses

Our noses are made of bamboo
We're the Long Noses
The Long Noses
Under the protection of the God Tingou

1st ACROBAT:	I can juggle candles.
2nd ACROBAT:	I can sing a song
3rd ACROBAT:	I can balance whirling plates
PASSEPARTOUT:	I can bang a gong
4th ACROBAT;	I can swallow down a sword
5th ACROBAT:	I can swallow four
6th ACROBAT:	I can imitate a flower
PASSEPARTOUT:	I can't stand much more

Our Long Noses were designed by Mrs Batulcar
Please give us the pleasure of asking who we are –

FOGG:	Who are you anyway?

We are
The Japanese Acrobatic Troup
Of the Honourable William Batulcar
This is
Our last performance before our departure
For the US of Americar
We're the Long Noses
The Long Noses
Our noses are made of bamboo
We're the Long Noses
The Long Noses
Under the protection
the very strong protection
Under the protection
And we need protection
Under the protection
Of the mighty god Tingou!

JUDY'S SONG

One woman works with her body bent in half
Plodding through paddy-fields planting rice
One woman lives on her feet for forty years
Working in a café called Paradise
One woman works mostly flat upon her back
Putting up with jeers and cruelties
But this woman works with a spikey scrubbing brush
Singing as she moves on hands and knees

Oh next time, next time when they ask me what I want to
be
I shall choose to be born as an albatross
And I'll sail over tourmaline seas
Yes next time, next time, when my reincarnation is due
I will choose to be born as a dolphin
And I'll swoop through the watery blue

One woman works with her body bent in half
Plodding through paddy-fields planting rice
One woman lives on her feet for forty years
Working in a cafe called Paradise
One woman works mostly flat upon her back
Putting up with jeers and cruelties
But this woman works with a spikey scrubbing brush
Singing as she moves on hands and knees

Oh last time, last time when they asked what I wanted
to be
Well I chose to be born as a woman
And I've lived on my hands and my knees
Oh but next time, next time, when they ask me what I
want to do
I shall choose to be be born as a vampire
And I'll frighten the crap out of you

PINEAPPLE MOON

There's a scent of Frangipani on the night breeze
The ocean looks as if it's wined and dined
And looking in your face I think you might seize
My heart my body my mind . . .

Pineapple moon
The Pacific breeze is balmy
Pineapple moon
Dangling from your palm tree
You are so fair
You are so mellow
Like an air
Played on cello
Pineapple moon
You're beginning to charm me
Pineapple moon
Dangling from your palm tree
You calm my heart
In every crisis
I'd like to cut
You into –
Pineapple Mooney Slices –

Pineapple moon
The Pacific breeze is balmy
Pineapple moon
Dangling from your palm tree
You smile at me
As if to say hello
Come to me
My little yellow fellow
Pineapple moon
Pineapple moon
I left my heart in your lagoon
Pineapple moon.

THE HAPPY-GO-LUCKY MINERS OF SAN FRANCISCO

GABBY HAYES
When you walked into the bar-room
I could tell it at a glance
I know you was a greenhorn
By the way you wore your pants.

Stranger, I better warn you
We're a rip-roaring bunch
With more whizzbang than a bullwhip!
Would you care to stay for lunch?

for

CHORUS

We're the happy-go-lucky miners of San Francisco
And we're even happier than usual to be here to say
Howdy Pardner to use the Western vernacular
We think you're spectacular
And we hope you'll stay
With the happy-go-lucky miners of San Francisco
We are simply delighted to greet you here today
Hang around and enjoy our hospitality
For your personality
Is brighter than the brightest
Happy-go-lucky San Francisco day!

1st MINER: Each day reveals new evidence of the
              profuse and intensified wealth of our
              favoured country.
2nd MINER: The metal is not silver alone – there are
              distinct ledges of auriferous ore.
3rd MINER: That's sure. A late discovery plainly
              evinces cinnabar.
4th MINER: The coarser metals are in gross abundance.
              Lately evidences of bituminous coal and a
              ligneous foundation have been detected –
GABBY: Heh heh heh – ain't you boys forgettin'?

107

CHORUS: Forgettin' what, old-timer?
GABBY: Forgettin' about our guest, that's all!

(CHORUS slap thighs)

Our apologies stranger, we was feelin' so happy-go-lucky,
We plumb got carried away.

We're the happy-go-lucky miners of San Francisco
And we're just delirious to be here to say
Howdy Pardner to use the Western vernacular
We think you're spectacular
And we hope you'll stay
With the happy-go-lucky miners of San Francisco
Who are simply delighted to greet you here today
Hang around and enjoy our hospitality
For your personality
Is brighter than the brightest
Righter than the rightest
Whiter than the whitest
Happy-go-lucky San Francisco miners' day!

GOLD RUSH BLUES

I gotta dirty man called Jimmy Whales
Acre of dirt under his toenails
He talks more dirt than a clergyman's parrot
But deep in Jimmy's dirt the gold is thirty six carat
Last night I caught him in a dirty situation
He grinned a yeller grin and gave a dirty explanation
I stared him in the eye
And gave him this reply:

I forgive you all my shame
When you're pannin' gold in my stream
First you stake your rightful claim

When you're pannin' for gold in my stream
You take a little rubble
You place it in your sieve
You shake it and you shake it
Till I just got to give
Oh I'm flying like an eagle in a gold rush dream
When you pannin' for gold in my stream

I know a lot of miners and I know what they like
They'd trade their mules for a lucky strike
But my man's solid gold from his boots to his shirt
Never stops shovellin' till he hits pay dirt
I saw a little gold mine, I asked who dug it?
He said: I don't know but I think I got the nugget
I stared at him again
And blurted out this refrain

I know exactly what I'm for
When you pannin' for gold in my stream
Yes I'll yield platinum and silver ore
When you pannin' for gold in my stream
When you swingin' your pickaxe
You always hit the seam
The gold shine so hot
I have to holler and scream
Yes
I'm higher than the sun in a gold rush dream
When you pannin' for gold in my stream
Oh please assay me
When you pannin' for gold in my stream
I'm jus' prospectin'
When you pannin' for gold in my stream

CIVILISE THIS LAND

When Columbus climbed up the Statue of Liberty
He gazed across America and said: Well I think it's grand.
I have a dream of true democracy,
So listen to the mighty vision I have planned:
We'll need polaroid bombs and calculating razors.
The sea's just a washing-machine for cleaning sand.
We're gonna have comic-books as bright as lasers.
Sooner or later we'll civilise this land.

Sooner or later
Sooner or later
We'll civilise this land

We're gonna sell you a Cadillac with lips.
We're gonna buy the Wailing Wall and give it to
Disneyland.
If you'd like a muttonburger that unzips
I'll meet you down at the Death Valley hot-dog stand.
Have you tried the jacuzzi in the Playboy submarine?
The Billie Holiday Inn has a rockin' band.
I sniff black coke in memory of James Dean –
I reckon we just about civilised this land.

Reckon we just about
Reckon we just about
Civilised this land.

We had some African slaves but we set 'em free.
Now all of the darkies call this the Motherland.
We'll invite Sammy Davis round for tea
And let Duke Ellington buy himself a concert grand.
Our destiny is manifest, everybody knows that's so –
If any of these Indian tribes gets out of hand
We'll civilise them like we civilised the buffalo.
From coast to coast we'll civilise this land.

From coast to coast
From coast to coast
We'll civilise this land.
With the maxim gun
And big John Wayne
And God's almighty hand
We're gonna civilise, civilise
Civilise this land.

SANDBANK SONG

Shipwrecked
On a sandback
Off the Southern
Coast of Ireland
On a soggy foggy day with you.
Signalling
To sailors
Off the Southern
Coast of Ireland
Simulating
Sanguine points of view.

And so here
We are.
So near
And yet so very very far.

Someone
Have a sandwich.
I'm so sorry
It's not sunny.
Sir, this sextant
Has been set all wrong.

Staring for a steamer
With the sunset
On the starboard
Singing such
A sad and silly song.

For we are

Shipwrecked
On a sandbank
Off the Southern
Coast of Ireland
On a soggy foggy day with you and you and you and you.
Signalling
To sailors
Off the Southern
Coast of Ireland
Simulating sanguine points of view-hoo-hoo-hoo-
hoooooooooo!

HOUDINI

An odd letter arrived from Amsterdam one day in the Seventies. The writer was a composer called Peter Schat and apparently he had set and performed my poem *To You* in enormous outdoor concerts. Now he wondered if I'd be interested in writing the libretto for an opera, probably on the theme of Eurydice. Since I was coming to the Rotterdam Poetry Festival, could we meet?

We met in a café and talked about Houdini – his skill, his imagination, his mother, his marriage. Peter, who I now know as a cross between Beethoven and Schoenberg, was enthusiastic, talking about magic and poetry and music and spectacle. Finally he picked up a cardboard match from a matchbook. He inked a cross on one side: "If it lands with that showing we will not make the Houdini opera". He inked a circle on the other side: "If it lands with that showing, we will not make the Houdini opera". Just as he threw it he bent the match in half, so that it landed on edge – and we both laughed at the small good luck trick.

This was the beginning of a very happy collaboration. Thanks to the Royal Dutch Opera we were able to visit each other's houses in London and Amsterdam and our families became good friends.

We became more and more fascinated with Houdini – his physical powers, his attacks on the spiritualists. Peter wrote most eloquent letters and one of them formed the basis of *The First Journey*, which follows.

Originally planned to be performed in the Vondelpark,

113

the opera became more and more ambitious. It called for the whole Concertgebouw Orchestra plus a steel band. We decided that it must be visually so eventful, with small and enormous tricks and escapes incorporated in the plot, that an audience which could hear nothing would still enjoy it.

It opened at the Carre, a variety theatre which Houdini played, was acclaimed and full for its whole run. It was shown at the Aspen Music Festival and then given a new production at Carre, better than the first.

The only drawback as a librettist was that, as usual in opera, many of the words could not be heard and my pleas for them to be printed out in subtitles were ignored. But the whole experience of working with Peter and the power of his music meant I had no regrets.

Composer: PETER SCHAT.

Performed: Carre Theatre, Amsterdam, 1977.

AFTER-LIFE

Life after death's a grisly fairy-tale
Told to produce obedient children.
We have one chance to work at building heaven,
And when we die, we're making room for someone.

After our death, what's left of us?
The results of our works and our lives –
Whatever we created for the people
And marks of our love and hate in those who survive.

One life – so take control of it,
Aim it towards the people's light
And that one life will soar through blue and white
Wonderfully as an albatross in flight.

For there is no heaven but the people.
Their strength and skill and vision
Are one billion times as overflowing
As the magic of a great magician.

MONEY IS THE ONLY MEDICINE

Money is the only medicine
To soothe the heart of man.
Money is the key to liberty
And the ticket to wonderland.
Money makes the heart beat stronger
Money kills the wildest fears.
Money helps you live much longer
And wipes away your tears.
Yes if you're hungry or in chains
Or simply tired and sick

There's an alternative to suicide –
Money does the trick.

A SONG OF LIBERATION

Padlocked in a barrel full of beer
And almost dying from the fumes –
He did not despair.

Lashed to the waterwheel
Tied to the sail of a windmill –
His skill did not desert him.

Chained to the pillar of a prison cell
Rivetted inside a metal boiler
Stuffed into the top of a roll-top desk
Sewn inside a giant sausage-skin –
He out-imagined his challenger.

Plunged into rivers, handcuffed and chained
Strapped to a crazy crib by mental nurses,
Tied to a cannon with a time fuse,
Hung upside down in the water torture cell,
In a Government mail pouch,
Even in the grave,
Even in the grave when he let himself be buried alive –

Even in the grave
His brain and body worked so perfectly
That he broke free from the grave.

And when the body of a man
Has been buried in the earth
And that body reaches up to the surface
That body reaches up towards the light,
Towards whatever shines –

116

Joy fills the people, magical joy.
Joy at the magic of his liberation,
Magic that touches the surface of your skin
With a magical shiver.
What is magic then?
What is magic? What is magic?

                    Beauty that takes you by surprise.

THE POLICE FORCE OF THE WORLD

The Police Force of the World
Holds all the world in awe
Even Christ could not escape
From the power of the law

The Police Force of the World
Has a million ears and eyes
And your friends are our informers
And your wife and your children our spies.

And we know your thoughts and we know your dreams
And we know your pettiest crimes
And the file on your life is mountainous
And we're only biding our time
Till we

Chain you and fasten you and fetter you and shackle you
Muzzle you and bridle you too
You'll be gagged and pinioned, handcuffed and tethered
Trussed and manacled too

In prisons and cages and dungeon cells
With bolts bars padlocks and walls
And the world will forget your existence
And you will forget the world

But you will always remember

The Police Force of the World
Which holds all the world in awe
Even Christ could not escape
From the power of the law

MEDICINE SHOW SONG

Anthropopo Patent Medicine
That's the stuff for you
Good for your blood
Good for your nerves
Good for your kidney and your bladder too

You can buy a dollar bottle for twenty-five cents
Prepared from the following ingredients:
Sasparilla, Yellow Dock and Prickly Ash,
Dandelion, Rhubarb and Sassafras.

Anthropopo if your blood's impure
Or your nerves are ragged or you need a cure
For rheumatism, pimples or skin disease,
Constipation, dandruff or housemaid's knees.
Antropopo will see you through
So buy a dozen bottles and God bless you!

THE FIRST JOURNEY

Once upon a time
Beyond the outer universe
On the far black meadows of nowhere
The human race assembled.
We made sure everyone was present and prepared.
Then we began our journey.

Under Niagaras of meteorites
Through jungle galaxies,
Over deserts of ammonia,
Along the million-year-deep canyons
Which gape between the stars,
We travelled together,
Towards the light,
Looking for a home.

On the planet Pluto
And on the planet Neptune
And on the planet Uranus
We froze in chemical oceans.
The sun no brighter than a match.

On the planet Saturn
The triple rings of silver
Dazzled and maddened us.

On the planet Jupiter
We were apples in the cider press
Of massive gravity.

On the planet Mars
We cried with thirst
And our tears were yellow dust.

On the planet Venus
We suffocated
Under four hundred miles
Of soaking clouds.

On the planet Mercury
We were offered
A choice of death by heat or cold.

But then we saw her
We saw our planet
Our earth
Our home

Let the people of the world
Shake off their chains and sing

There is no heaven but the Earth
There is no heaven but the People

Let the people of the world
Shake off their chains
And dance
And dance towards the light
Towards whatever shines.

SPEEDWELL

The summit of the speedwell flower
Opens from green
Into an eye of blue and white
Staring towards the light,
Towards whatever shines.

A new-born baby's eyes
Turn towards the light,
Towards whatever shines.

A new-born baby's hands
Reach out towards the light,
Towards whatever shines.

120

UPPENDOWN MOONEY

This was an odd piece about a village of animals. The Squire was a polar bear who in one scene raped a swallow. There were some dancing fleas and the narrator was a hedgehog called Mad Gus. Yes, a Welfare State job.

I'd known Welfare State International people – Boris and Maggie Howarth, John and Sue Fox, for some years and I would have joined them if I hadn't been deep in debt. They are my favourite theatre company of all time. Those who don't know their work should read their handbook – *Engineers of the Imagination* (Methuen) and go to any of their gigs. Sometimes they perform enormous spectacles like *The Burning Down of the Houses of Parliament* or *Raising the Titanic*, sometimes small ceremonies like naming ceremonies for children or weddings, sometimes barn dances or feasts. They have the freest imaginations I've met and few equals as makers of beauty.

The first performance of *Uppendown Mooney* was on a nilltop a few miles outside Lancaster. The audience approached a large tent through a maze of sculptured and painted images. We sat in the dark tent and listened as the hedgehog introduced the piece. Then one side of the tent rolled up and we saw the stage – a complete landscape stretching down into a green valley and up to another hilltop. As the play progressed the landscape darkened. (A phoenix was the most important, healing character.) At the play's end there appeared on the opposite hillside, in flames, the image of an enormous phoenix.

Composers: BORIS HOWARTH and GREG STEPHENS.

Performed: Hilltop, Wennington and tour by Welfare State
International, Engineers of the Imagination,
1978.

SONG IN SPACE

When man first flew beyond the sky
He looked back into the world's blue eye.
Man said: What makes your eye so blue?
Earth said: The tears in the oceans do.
Why are the seas so full of tears?
Because I've wept so many thousand years.
Why do you weep as you dance through space?
Because I am the mother of the human race.

THE WOMAN OF WATER

There once was a woman of water
Refused a wizard her hand
So he took the tears of a statue
And the weight from a grain of sand
And he squeezed the sap from a comet
And the height from a cypress tree
And he drained the dark from midnight
And he charmed the brains from a bee
And he soured the mixture with thunder
And stirred it with ice from hell
And the woman of water drank it down
And she changed into a well

There once was a woman of water
Who was changed into a well
And the well smiled up at the wizard
And down down down that old wizard fell. . . .

LOVE IN A NEST

Look, look what I've found –
Smooth and warm and round.
I love what I've found –
Smooth and warm and round.
Love, love all around –
Smooth and warm and round.
The world's all goldeny ground –
Smooth and warm and round.

TO A POSTMAN

I used to think bean soup
Was simply bean soup
Just another flavour
I was vaguely in favour
Then you came in my kitchen
Grinding black pepper
Shaking that dry salt
Don't say it was my fault

Oh you saved me from the flu and the man from the Pru
And the Christians and the rising damp.
Mister Postman – lick my stamp.

SHJOM

The egg of the phoenix
And the month of miracles
Crack wide open
Shjom

Shjom comes back
With all the brass of spring
Shjom comes back
On his benevolent wings

The penny-whistle stars
And the earth's great drum
Change their music
Shjom

Shjom comes back
Shjom comes back
Let us welcome Shjom

THE SQUIRE'S CURSE

By the beauty queen with the twisted neck on the floor of
      the Stock Exchange
I put a curse on you
By the daily paper which prints the headline: You are in
      my power
I put a curse on you
By the beautiful hands of the artist designing a
      thumbscrew in stainless steel
I put a curse on you
By the Naafi clerk who chalks Get Well Soon on the side of
      the Black Death bomb

I put a curse on you
By the embryo found in the elephant's foot umbrella stand
By the nine times table and the fungoid slum and the
               paranoid submarine
By the terrible mating of Action Man and Barbie Doll
I put a curse on you
By the prison covered in shit and piss
By the palace covered in icing sugar
By the human race which made all this
I put a curse on you

BELLY SLAPPING DANCE

Well a football's here to be kicked
And a cricket ball's here to be bowled
And the sun is here to paint the atmosphere
In various shades of gold

Babies love woolly bears
Children love jammy tarts
A girl and a bloke who can see the joke
Love their interlocking parts

Well Pharaoh is meant to sink and drown
And Lazarus is meant to rise
And the moon it seems is meant to use its beams
To tickle every animal's thighs

Well Tarzan always gets Jane
But Romeo always gets killed
And we'd like to say in a similar way
That everyone's bellies get filled

For food is made to be scoffed
And booze is made to be swilled
So give us a cough and we'll dance off
To get our bellies filled.

SOMEONE AT MY DOOR

"Why are you knocking at my door?"
"I come in peace, and I come in war."
"Do you come with a knife or a begging-bowl?"
"I come to stare into your soul."
"Come in, I'll devour you like the rest."
"Here – take my heart from out of my breast."

HUSH LITTLE BABY

Hush little baby full of blood
I know you're longing to explode.
But if you'll sleep and rest your wings
Papa's going to get you everything.
If everything is not enough
Papa's going to get you twice as much.
If twice as much is far too small
Papa's going to get you ten times tall.
If ten times tall is much too thin
Papa's going to get you a thousand thing.
If a thousand gets less and less
Papa's going to get you a million piece.
If a million piece is quickly gone
Papa's going to get until Kingdom come.
Hush little baby full of blood
I know you're longing to explode
But if you'll sleep and rest your wings
Papa's going to get you everything.

WE'VE GOT PRIDE (Song of the Fleas)

They say we're –
                    Dirty – Mucky – Filthy – Yucky –
Why should we care if we're despised and ignored?
They say we're –
                    Scruffy – Itchy – Boney – Titchy –
But we've been chosen by Lord Claude!

So we're full of pride today.
What is it like to feel such pride?
Well that's rather hard to say
But it's like having a pint of warm treacle
Poured into your inside!
Pride!   We've got pride!
Pride!   We've got pride!
Pride!   We've got pride!

LATE AFTERNOON

Late Afternoon
Sun shone yellow
I took the path to the well

Late afternoon
Sun shone yellow
Shadows were growing
I took the path to the well

Late afternoon
Sun shone yellow
Shadows were growing
I wore my white dress
I took the path to the well

Late afternoon
Sun shone yellow
Shadows were growing
I wore my white dress
Blackberries glowing
I took my path to the well

Late afternoon
Sun shone yellow
Shadows were growing
I wore my white dress
Blackberries glowing
I was trapped by brambles
I took the path to the well

The sun cast shadows on my white dress
Hands full of blackberries I stood among the brambles
Late afternoon
Late afternoon
I took the path to the well.

THE WHITE DEER

An adaptation of Thurber's classic for children. Most of the songs were simply arrangements of Thurber's astonishing prose. *Doves And Roses* was the simple culminating song.

Composer: ILONA SEKACZ.

Performed: Unicorn Theatre for Children, 1978.

DOVES AND ROSES

I dreamed about a Princess
Long away and far ago
I dreamed about a princess
And her voice was lovely
As sunlight on the snow.

And she sang:

Doves and roses
Doves and roses
Golden trumpets play
Horses shake their shining manes
As we ride away

A hedgehog stops and scratches his head
Sunflowers watch in wonder
Swallows dive from the blue-eyed skies
And a wonderful waterfall doubles its thunder.
Golden rain drops begin to fall
Silvery fountains play
And our horses are stepping out sturdily
As we ride away

Doves and roses
Doves and roses
Shining all the way
Red and white and yellow wine
For the wedding day

Doves and roses
Doves and roses
Doves and roses
Doves and roses.

PEER GYNT

This was a verse version with plenty of songs taking the place of long speeches. Ibsen wrote it when he was feeling happy, living in Frascati and probably drinking a lot of local wine if you ask me. He didn't intend it for the theatre and when he found out it was going to be staged suggested cutting down Act Four and replacing it with a series of tableaux. But I didn't want to cut down the number of scenes or even the number of speeches, rather the length of some of the scenes.

Gordon MacDougall, who commissioned the version for Oxford Playhouse, said at one point he was dubious about the scene with monkeys. I said, hang on, you don't pass up the chance of a scene with monkeys. In our version Peer gets chased up a tree by a lion and is just saying "You missed me, yah boo" or words to that effect, when a whole load of monkeys start throwing shit on his head from the top of the tree. Image of the human condition, halfway up a tree with a lion down below and monkeys throwing shit from up above. All right then, it's not an image for the human condition.

As usual with my versions of foreign plays, I worked from a literal translation, this one by Karin Bamborough who is half Norwegian and was thus able to read me passages in the original and supply me with notes and criticism.

In *The Song of the Thoughts* as in several other lyrics in the book, I've used half-rhymes. This can be very effective in creating a spooky or odd incomplete feel, but you do get the odd attack from critics who've never heard of half-rhyme or assonance (not having met Auden or Owen) and so think you're trying for a full rhyme and missing through carelessness. I always send them a polite note explaining what I'm doing in the hope of being understood next time.

Composer: NICK BICAT.

Performed: Oxford Playhouse, 1980.

GREAT WHITE STALLION

great white stallion
great white stallion
as you fly with your white-flowing mane
and your horseshoes as golden as sunshine
and your bridle as silver as rain

great white stallion
great white stallion
as you gallop your sky shaking way
with your saddle of african leather
do you know who's your rider today?

peer gynt! peer gynt!
in his shimmering cloak lined with silk beneath.
peer gynt! peer gynt!
with his spanish sabre in its scarlet sheath.
what grace! what style!
what a fearsome frown!
what a magical smile!
and the crowd is proud to shout aloud:
peer gynt! peer gynt!

peer gynt! peer gynt!
all the gentlemen throw up their hats and cheer.
peer gynt! peer gynt!
all the ladies curtsey to magnificent peer.
and each of them
gets a golden coin
or a valued gem.
and the crowd is proud to shout aloud:
peer gynt! peer gynt!

ME FIRST (TROLL SONG)

a little dutch boy saw a hole in a dyke
so he scrambled on his daddy's motorbike
he didn't hang around to see the damn dam burst,
he zoomed off to germany yelling: "me first!"

me first
when they ladle out the honey
me first
when they handing out the money
if they're standing in line
i'll be round the back door
me first, me first
till there isn't any more
if i'm gonna be first
i gotta be fast
only suckers
finish last
so i'll do my best
and i'll do my worst.
the result?
me first, me first, me first.

sir philip sydney on the battlefield lay
he was badly wounded in the heat of the day.
he saw a fellow-soldier who was dying of thirst
so he grabbed the guy's heineken yelling: me first!

me first
when they ladle out the honey
me first
when they handing out the money
if they're standing in line
i'll be round the back door
me first, me first
till there isn't any more

if i'm gonna be first
i gotta be fast
only suckers
finish last
so i'll do my best
and i'll do my worst.
the result?
me first, me first, me first.

jesus christ came to earth, it's a matter of fact.
with a box office smashing magical act.
but the cross wasn't scripted, let alone rehearsed
so he zoomed back to heaven's gate yelling: "me first!"

me first
when they ladle out the honey
me first
when they handing out the money
if they're standing in line
i'll be round the back door
me first, me first
till there isn't any more
if i'm gonna be first
i gotta be fast
only suckers finish last
so i'll do my best
and i'll do my worst
the result?
me first, me first, me first.

it's so strange
the human being
strange
the human being
strangest
the human being
when it's you
being human.

can we change
the human being?
change
its way of seeing
change its
strange way of seeing
so the
human being
stops
being human?

delicate surgery
technically trouble-free
trollvision installation
an exquisite operation

i will slash your right eye
with a herring knife
and you'll see the beauty
of your beautiful wife
we can change
the human being
change
its way of seeing
change its
strange way of seeing
so the
human being
stops –

peer gynt thought that he needed no guide
he reckoned he had henrik ibsen on his side.
but peer got shattered by a stun-gun burst
of me first! me first! me first!

me first
when we're duffing up a stranger
me first
when there isn't any danger
if they're queueing to kick

him down on the floor
me first, me first
till he's covered with his gore
if i'm gonna hit first
i gotta hit fast
only suckers
finish last
so i'll do my best
and i'll do my worst.
the result?
me first! me first! me first!

CUTTING DOWN THE TREE

well i know that you're tough
hey!
but you're not tough enough
hey!
i know that you're wearing a solid steel bark
but i'm going to cut you down before dark
hey!
and that's how.

now my muscles may ache
hey!
but i'm making you shake
hey!
you're welcome to curse me as much as you please
but i'm going to cut you down to your knees
hey!
and that's how.

138

I TRAVELLED ON SKIS

i travelled on skis
i travelled alone
they said: "where are you going?"
i said: "i'm going home."

I SHALL SURVIVE

on the first day of my journey
wearing no shoes on my feet
my pockets were all empty
my bed was a ditch
and i never had enough to eat

i shall survive
in the golden hive
otherwise what's the use?
life is my home
in the honeycomb
but death is lemon juice.

on the second day of my journey
lady luck travelled with me
i greeted her politely
she treated me well
and my fortune changed miraculously.

i shall survive
in the golden hive
otherwise what's the use?
life is my home
in the honeycomb
but death is lemon juice.

on the third day of my journey
seeing where the big money lay
i rounded up some africans
put them on a boat
and shipped them off to charleston bay.

i shall survive
in the golden hive
otherwise what's the use?
life is my home
in the honeycomb
but death is lemon juice.

on the fourth day of my journey
slavery was in the past
so i built my blacks a schoolhouse
gave them money and food
and they worked for me twice as fast.

i shall survive
in the golden hive
otherwise what's the use?
life is my home
in the honeycomb
but death is lemon juice.

I LOCKED THE DOOR

i locked the door of paradise
and pocketed the key.
i put out to sea 'neath stormy skies
while on the shore the lovely eyes
of women wept for me.

i sailed her south for many a day
with dolphins at her stern

and where the lofty palm trees sway
around a blue and brilliant bay
i let my good ship burn.

you sparkle like some magic brew
of potent palm tree wine.
goat cheese is wonderful, that's true
but not as nourishing as you.
anitra – let us dine.

KING APIS

they called him king apis
but king apis went and died
now they call him mummy
because he's mummified

king apis built sphinxes
and slaughtered lots of turks
put up many pyramids
and other public works

and i am king apis
it's clear as the moon
if you don't believe me
you will bloody soon

king apis went hunting
he squatted on the soil
where my grandfather
used to sweat and toil

the cornfield flourished
later i was born
and i ate the royally
fertilised corn

so i am king apis
it's clear as the moon
if you don't believe me now
you will bloody soon

now isn't it shameful?
isn't it unpleasant?
by birth i am king apis
but they treat me like a peasant

so tell me what to do
to change my sorry fate
so that everyone knows
i'm king apis the great

for he is king apis
it's clear as the moon
if you don't believe him now
you will bloody soon

why don't you build sphinxes
and slaughter lots of turks
build lots of pyramids
and other public works?

but buildings won't help me
to be worshipped as the great
king apis of egypt in
his mummified state

why not take a rope
and try suicide,
so you can be properly
mummified.

yes i'll take a rope
and try suicide,
so i can be properly mummified.

THE EMPEROR OF SELF

he is the emperor of self.
why's he the emperor of the self?
because he's the emperor of the self.
long live the emperor of the self.

he is the emperor of the self.
why's he the emperor of the self?
because he's the emperor of the self.
long live the emperor of the self.

long live the emperor
long live the self
long live the emperor of the self

long live the emperor
long live the self
long live the emperor of the self!

THE PIG SONG

when i was out in san francisco
the devil just happened along.
he wanted to clown like the others
but he hadn't a joke or a song.
he hadn't got the head for the highwire,
and he didn't have the legs for a jig
so he said: i'll perform you my one-man-play –
the life and death of a pig.

when i was out in san francisco
the devil's reputation was big.
he strode on the stage in a scarlet cape
and underneath was hidden a pig.

whenever the devil stuck a pin in the pig
it grunted about its life,
but it gave the finest squeal of all
when he cut its throat with a knife.

when i was out in san francisco
the critics were all of one mind.
the devil was a porcine impersonator
of a most inferior kind.
his dying squeal they found completely unreal,
his grunting was a load of rot.
and if *you* misjudge your audience
you'll get what that poor devil got.

THE SONG OF THE THOUGHTS

peer gynt.
you should have given us
hands and feet
but we are the thoughts
you never thought.

we should have risen up
high in the air
but we're just stones and
we're stuck down here.

we are dry and withered leaves
riding on the wings of the past
we're the answers to the questions
you never bothered to ask.

we are the tears you never shed.
we could have melted
the spikes in your head.
those icicle nails

144

are fixed in your brain
and now it's too late
to melt them down again.

we are the deeds
that you should have done.
when we tried to break out
you forced us back down.
we rotted away
in the dungeons of your heart
now we only exist
as poison in your throat.

SLEEP AND SMILE

sleep and smile in your sleep my dear
i'll watch over my little peer.

the boy sat on his mother's lap
he sat upon her lap
his whole life through.

the boy looked in his mother's eyes
he looked into her eyes
his whole life through.

the boy lay at his mother's breast
lying at her breast
his whole life through.

the boy curled up in his mother's heart
he curled up in her heart
his whole life through.
sleep and smile in your sleep my dear
i'll watch over my little peer.

i'll watch over my little peer
sleep and dream in your sleep my dear.

MOWGLI'S JUNGLE

An adaptation of Kipling's Mowgli stories, which I loved as a child. It was a story about a boy growing up among wolves who found that he was not really a wolf and not really a man.
Nearly all the songs were by Kipling, but I introduced one by Edward Lear (*Calico Pie*) and one song for the widow who adopts Mowgli.

The acting, direction and design were fine, but although I'd asked for actors with strong voices and a good ear, the singing was mostly substandard. Which was a shame, because the music was marvellous.

Composer: MIKE WESTBROOK.

Performed: Contact Theatre, Manchester. 1981.

THE WIDOW'S SONG

My husband was strong
My husband was warm
His loving was
A thunderstorm
But a fever came
And took him by the hand
Now he is dancing,
Dancing, dancing
With the ghosts in Ghostland

My baby could stand
My baby could dance
His hands and legs
Like little plants
But a tiger came
And took him by the hand
Now he is dancing,
Dancing, dancing
With the ghosts in Ghostland

And now I am poor
As poor as a stone
All day and night
Alone alone
Let dreams tonight
Take me by the hand
And I'll go dancing,
Dancing, dancing
With the ghosts
With my lovely ghosts
With my lovely ghosts in Ghostland

SOMETHING DOWN THERE IS CRYING

A half-hour TV play about a rock singer having a
breakdown during a posh party.

It was sung and acted by the red-hot Elkie Brooks. We
spent an evening with a piano and a bottle of whisky
planning more exploits. I remember she was very
interested in food and I was going to write her an LP's
worth of songs about grub. But suddenly she got extremely
famous and nothing ever came of it.

Composer: ANDY ROBERTS.

Performed: BBC TV, 1981.

SOMETHING DOWN THERE IS CRYING

You invited me to climb your golden stairs
And join you in your diamond suite.
They say the air up there is brandy mist
And you're swooning in your body's heat
For me —

But

Something down there is crying.
Something down there's in chains.
Something down there is crying
And it cuts right through my brains.

You bought yourself a playboy Heaven,
I guess it cost you most of your soul.
I heard about your millionaire loving
And how you lose total control
For me —

But

Something down there is crying.
Something down there in chains.
Something down there is crying
And it cuts right through my brains . . .

SORRY BOUT THAT

Truth is a diamond
A diamond is hard
You don't exist
Without a Barclaycard

Well I'm sorry bout that
Yes I'm sorry bout that
Even South African cops
Do the sorry bout that.

I was sucking that whisky
Before I could crawl
Gonna get dead drunk
At the money suckers ball

And I'm sorry bout that
Yes I'm sorry bout that
Mother, I need that booze
And I'm sorry bout that.

Wanta be your clown
Wanta be your cow
Just touch me with your money
Come on, slip it to me now.

Sorry bout that
Sorry bout that
I'm the tart with a heart of lead
And I'm sorry bout that.

Wanta be your joker
Wanta be your whore
Wanta be the boot-scraper
Outside your door.

Sorry about that
Yes I'm sorry bout that
Well I know how you use your boots
And I'm sorry bout that.

Wanta be your bog
Wanta be your bride
Wanta be your happy little
Suicide

Sorry bout that

Sorry bout that
Get me to the churchyard on time
sorry bout that

I know you cut your conscience
Into Kenno-meat chunks
You got elected
To the House of Drunks.

Well I'm sorry bout that
So sorry bout that
You'll never have to think again
And I'm sorry bout that

You can do the Skull
Or the Diplomat
But I do the dance called
The Sorry Bout That.

Sorry bout that
Sorry bout that
If I step on your blue suede soul
Well I'm sorry bout that

Do the Mighty Whitey
Or the Landlord Rat
I'll keep grooving
To the Sorry Bout That

Well I'm sorry bout that
So sorry bout that
They make me dance with pistols
And ten to one I'm sorry bout that

I saw Money walking
Down the road
Had claws like an eagle
And a face like a toad

Sorry bout that
Sorry bout that

It may come to killing, if it does
Well I'm sorry bout that

I know your face baby
Well I've seen it before
Putting on your make-up
For the Third World War

Sorry bout that
Sorry bout that
Someone set the world on fire
Well I'm sorry bout that

I know your name baby
I can smell your breath
I know your name lover
Your name is –

Rio Tinto Zinc
Barclays Bank
Phoenix Assurance
Imperial Tobacco
Rothschild and Sons
British Petroleum
Distillers Company
Reed International
British Leyland
ICI
ITT
CIA
BBC
Metal Box Company
Xerox Guinness EMI
United Dominions Trust
Computer Technology
Sotheby's Christies
Wimpey and Laing

Yes, yes yes yes yes yes yes

I know your name baby

Yes I can smell your breath
You all got the same damn family name –
Your name is death

And I see all of your names
Written in Flames.

YOU MUST BELIEVE ALL THIS

This was a TV play for children based loosely on Charles Dickens's wonderfully funny *Holiday Romance*, about four children who become story-tellers. In the play they produce and sell a magazine of their work entitled *You Must Believe All This*.

The play was produced by Sue Birtwistle and directed by Richard Bramall and I was delighted with it. It's published as a stage play to be performed by adults and children by Thames Methuen.

Composer: NICK BICAT and ANDREW DICKSON.

Performed: December 24th 1981, Thames Television.

YOU MUST BELIEVE ALL THIS

Wonderful adventures,
Pirates, blood and whales.
Magical, tragical
Fairy tales.
Exciting fighting
And cannibal stew.
You must believe all this,
Because all this is true.

You must believe all this.
It isn't tommy rot.
You must believe all this,
It will teach you such a lot.
The one magazine
No grown-up should miss.
You must believe,
You must believe,
You must believe all this!

Marvellous encounters,
Horrible mistakes,
Mutiny, laughter and wedding cakes.
Delightful, frightful
And written for you.
You must believe all this
Because all this is true.

You must believe all this,
For it's sweet and yet sensational.
You must believe all this:
It's also educational.
The one magazine
No grown-up can miss,
You must believe,
You must believe all this.

NOT A VERY CHEERFUL SONG I'M AFRAID

There was a gloomy lady,
With a gloomy duck, and a gloomy drake,
And they all three wandered gloomily,
Beside a gloomy lake,
On a gloomy, gloomy, gloomy, gloomy, gloomy, gloomy,
        day

Now underneath that gloomy lake,
The gloomy lady's gone,
But the gloomy duck and the gloomy drake
Swim on and on,
On a gloomy, gloomy, gloomy, gloomy, gloomy, gloomy,
            day.

THE WILD ANIMAL SONG CONTEST

Asked to write a play about peace to tour London primary schools in termtime and parks in school holidays by the Unicorn Theatre for Children, it took time to find a way. I didn't know how to explain how I felt about war to kids of that age. In the end I chose a rigged song contest as a metaphor for cut-throat competition and the forming of a rock group as a metaphor for cooperation – cooperation being the only true basis for peace.

The set was simple – a huge TV set and a dressing-room table with light bulbs. To the contest came an eagle from the USA, a bear from the USSR, a seedy lion from England and a beautiful black giraffe from Africa. Only the giraffe imagined the contest could be about singing a beautiful song. Eventually she discovered that the contest was fixed by the organiser, a penguin called Debit, and persuaded the other animals to join together as a group. Even then they had to learn to take turns at the mike.

The costumes were bright and light, each actor's face being fully visible without losing the beauty of the animals (for instance the giraffe actress's face appeared in an oval cut halfway up the giraffe's neck). This caused none of the anticipated double focus problems. It's the mediaeval solution to animal costumes and I believe the best one. The bear actor's head was freely seen directly under the upper jaw of the bear's head etc.

Because the play had to work outdoors there was a high proportion of songs and the whole show lasted about 55 minutes. I think it was one of my best efforts and hope to expand it into a full-length show soon.

158

Composer: ANDREW DICKSON.

Performed: Unicorn Theatre for Children on tour in London, 1982.

WHEN THE EAGLE SMILES

Now all you young animals gather round
Listen what the eagle is laying down
If you've any sort of ears then you've certainly heard
That the golden eagle is the number one bird
And a wave of terror rolls for miles and miles
      When the eagle smiles.

And what is the eagle smiling about
As she rules the land and sea?
What is the eagle smiling about?
She smiles because she's free
Free
Free . . .

My claws are carved like crooked little spears
My eyes of anger have never shed tears
I stand on the mountain in my golden cloak
Then I dive on my victim like a thunderstroke
And a wave of terror rolls for miles and miles
      When the eagle smiles

And what is the eagle smiling about
As she rules the land and sea?
What is the eagle smiling about?
She smiles because she's free
Free
Free . . .

When I get em in my sights goodbye to hope
The seal, the lamb and the antelope
My beak is designed to rip and tear
And that's what makes me Queen of the Air
And a wave of terror rolls for miles and miles
      When the eagle smiles.

And what is the eagle smiling about
As she rules the land and sea?
What is the eagle smiling about?
She smiles because she is free
Free
Free
And you'd smile if you were me
Don't you wish that you were
Free like me?

THE DANCING BEAR

My father was a bear who danced
To a drummer's lively beat
The people crowded round to see
My father stomp his feet

In outposts of Siberia
And at the Moscow Fair
The people stood with goggly eyes
To see a dancing bear

Was he a furry genius
Blessed with a dancer's brain?
Oh no he was a frightened bear
And he danced out of pain

His master made him stand upon
A box of red hot steel
Till when my father heard the drum
The painful heat he'd feel

And I am angry to my soul
About my father's fate
And that is why I do not dance
And that is why I hate . . .

THE CAMELEOPARD (the giraffe's song)

There was a leopard
There was a leopard in the forest
His coat was the colour of the sun
There was a leopard
There was a leopard in the forest
Had a hundred black spots all different
There was a leopard
His eyes were sleepy flames
And he was lonely as a shooting star
As a shooting star

There was a camel
There was a camel in the desert
Her coat was the colour of the earth
There was a camel
There was a camel in the desert
She had a muddled mind but a perfect heart
There was a camel
Her eyes were shining coal
And she was lonely as an empty bird's nest
As an empty nest

Now the sun was walking down the sky one day
He squeezed a fat cloud till it had to rain
The rain collected up in a bowl of sand
Between the forest and the desert

And the leopard was thirsty
Colour of the sun
And the camel was dirty
Colour of the earth
So the leopard came to drink
And the camel came to bathe
In deep cool of the pool

There was a leopard
There was a leopard in the forest
His coat was the colour of the sun

There was a camel
There was a camel in the desert
Her coat was the colour of the earth
And they met in the middle
Of the cool cool pool
And they stared at each other
Eyes of flame
Eyes of coal
And all their loneliness
Was burned and washed away

The giraffe is the child of their loving
The giraffe is the child of their love
The giraffe is the child of their loving
The giraffe is the child of their love.

ROGAN THE LION'S ROARING SONG

You've seen me on golden syrup tins
And movies by MGM
I appeared with a witch and a wardrobe
And I didn't think much of them
I'm an aristocrat and a gentleman
I never blow bubble gum
And I talk real posh, for I never say gosh
Or belly or blimey or bum

> I go ROAR
> That's right royal roaring
> I go ROAR
> It never gets boring
> My ROAR
> My wonderful ROAR
> I go ROAR
> I roar like a river
> I go ROAR

And my enemies shiver
At my ROAR
My wonderful super-charged ROAR

Now I had a job in a circus once
And I didn't care much for that
For they didn't treat me like a king
But a musclebound pussy cat
Now I'm not so young as I used to was
But you'd better not forget
Though my teeth are falling and my mane is balding
There's life in the old lion yet

I go ROAR (etc)

I used to go zebra-bashing
Or take a little deer for lunch
But now I'd rather be given a tin
Of Kit-e-Kat or Whiskas to munch
But I haven't given up slaughtering
I murder now and again
I might bite in half some young giraffe
And you'll know I'm still in business when

I go ROAR
That's right royal roaring
I go ROAR
It never gets boring
My ROAR
My wonderful ROAR
I go ROAR
I roar like a river
I go ROAR
And my enemies shiver
At my ROAR
My wonderful super-charged walloping
thatchery
ROOOOOOOOOAR!

THE TRAVELS OF LANCELOT QUAIL

Over the years performer and pig-farmer Jamie Proud
created a mythical character who rejoiced in the name of
Lancelot Icarus Handyman Quail who was chased and
gave chase through the multi-coloured landscapes of
several Welfare State International shows. The State
decided to use Quail again when they were asked to
mount a celebration for Wales in Caerphilly Castle in 1984.
Boris Howarth told of the events he planned in the castle,
around the castle, on the water and in the air. I made
some lyrics to fit his story. Unfortunately the money for
the project was withdrawn at the last moment so the show
collapsed. But I want to keep these . . .

The *Lament for the Welsh Makers* is, of course, based on
William Dunbar's *Lament for the Makers*, with its refrain:
"Timor mortis conturbat me". I used the same model again
in *We* for my *Lament for the Jazz Makers*, which appears later
in the book.

Published: Welfare State International, 1984.

THE WONDROUS GENEALOGY OF LANCELOT QUAIL

My mother was the Beauty
My father was the Beast
I'm Mister Hairy Universe
To say the bloody least.

My granny was the mountains
My grandpa was the mud
I was born in a bonfire
With gunpowder blood.

Great-Grandpa was the North Pole
Great-granny was the Equator
They may freeze me now
But they'll fry me later.

Great-Great-Granny was the Amazon
Great-Great-Grandpa was the Nile
So my head is full of jungles
And rocker crocodiles.

Great-great-great grandpa lives on Pluto
Great-great-great grannie comes from Mars
I was born to desperado
As the outlaw of the stars.

And if anyone should ask you
Who made this mighty song
Tell them — Lancelot Quail's
The Wonder of Wales
But now that poor boy's gone.

THE BOASTING SONG OF LANCELOT QUAIL

Gather round me children and buy us an ale
And I'll tell you of the greatitude of Lancelot Quail.
He's a human steam-roller, you can take him apart,
He's got a monster in his belly and a baby in his heart
He's an angel with horns and a flicker-knife tail
And he goes by the name of Lancelot Quail.

He's the gas attack songster with only one lung
But he can croonerize you everything Vera Lynn sung.
He's the spit-and-run comedian with only one joke
But he throws it like a hammer and it flattens the folk.
He can recite the Daily Mail in braille
Which is greatly to the glorybeans of Lancelot Quail.

He friendlied the Space Tramp in Uttermost Space,
Fell back to earth and made a crater in its face.
He can do the Parliament bonnyfire dance,
He's the big-dream hunter just waiting for his chance.
The cops pay his bail to keep him out of jail
And he judges the judges does Lancelot Quail.

He gets visions regular as you buy milk –
Waterfalls of honey in landscapes of silk.
But the highest vision that ever thrust home
Was Morwena the mermaid with a corally comb.
You should hear him wail for that shiny female –
Swim to the loving arms of Lancelot Quail!

He dallied and dillied with the devil one night
Till he turned into a Strongman Hermaphrodite.
He's been for a ride in a submarine
And the Queen kicked him out of the Serpenteen.
Bureaucrats pale when they hear him rail –
Lord Mayors are the breakfast food of Lancelot Quail.

The Saliva Surfer and the Credible Hunk,
He crossed the Milky Way in a rocket made of junk.
He ghosted for the people and he wooed them with food
He visited Birmingham and stripped the city nude.

167

Through the hail and gales
Of the vales of Wales
He's on the tail
Of his fishtail Grail
He's the super-sad
Golden-eyed
Happy-go-horrified
He's your own, your very own,
One is one and all alone,
One and lonely Lancelot Quail!

THE GARDEN PARTY SONG

The lawns have been immaculately manicured
Dark green, light green, in alternating lines
The guests have all been vetted by policemen
They all display cards which confirm their identities
Some of them come from government departments
Some of them come from the aristocracy
Some from the Church and some from the Army
Everyone is somebody or married to somebody
Several of the ministers are followed by their bodyguards
As they stroll on the immaculate lawns.

     Safe   safe
Delicate cakes and cups of tea
     Safe   safe
Flowers all over the millinery
     Safe   safe
     Safe   safe
Safe as houses
Safe as parcels
Safe as the civil service
Safe as castles

     Garden party afternoon.

FAREWELL SONG

Gravely farewell Caerphilly
Farewell island of my birth
Farewell animals and people
Of the famous planet Earth

Nothing much
I have accumulated
So
Nothing much
Take back from me
I am gone, you'll hardly notice
You felt nothing much for me

So

Gravely farewell Caerphilly
Farewell island of my birth
Farewell animals and people
Of the famous planet Earth

VOYAGE SONG IN QUEST OF THE MERMAID MORWENA

As the valley wind tickles the little grass
So let the hull of my good ship pass
Over the water's greeny glass
So let the hull of my good ship pass

To where the water slides
Reluctantly
From her wonder-loving
Breasted body
I want to slide every part of her

Over every part of me
One time serious
And one time funny
Oh mermaid love
You shine like golden money
You shine like the secret
Of the place among the rocks
Where the two rivers marry in spray
You shine like a woman
Like the flesh of a woman
Or a fish or a woman
Like the skin of a dolphin
Or a dancing woman
Or a salmon jumping
Or a mocking woman
Or a seal in heaven
Or a full-hearted woman
Or a full-hearted woman
And I'd journey to the bottom to the top of the sky
To get my love on you
To get your love on me
To get my love in you
To get your love in me

As the valley wind tickles the little grass
So let the hull of my good ship pass
Over the water's greeny glass
So let the hull of my good ship pass

THE RIDDLE AT THE CROSSROADS

A man and a woman
On the mountains made moan:
We cannot speak
A language of our own.
Our children are stolen,
Our land, our everything.
Name us the devil who has done this thing?

LAMENT FOR THE WELSH MAKERS

WILLIAM DUNBAR sang piteously
When he mourned for the Makers of poetry.
He engraved their names with his commentary –
Timor mortis conturbat me.

DUNBAR, I'm Scot-begotten too,
But I would celebrate a few
Welsh masters of word-wizardry –
The fear of death moves inside me.

"After the feasting, silence fell."
ANEIRIN knew how the dead smell.
Now he has joined their company –
The fear of death moves inside me.

TALIESIN, born of earth and clay,
Primroses, the ninth wave's spray
And nettle flowers, where is he?
The fear of death moves inside me.

LLYWARCH'S sons numbered twenty-four.
Each one was eaten by the war.
He lived to curse senility.
The fear of death moves inside me.

TALHEARN and AROFAN,
AFAN FERDDIG and MORFRAN
Are lost, with all their poetry.
The fear of death moves inside me.

MERDDIN sang, a silver bell,
But from the battlefield he fell
Into a deep insanity.
The fear of death moves inside me.

GWALCHMAI, who sang of Anglesey
And a girl like snowfall on a tree
And lions too, lies silently –
The fear of death moves inside me.

CYNDDELW's balladry was sold
For women's kisses and men's gold.
His shop is shut permanently.
The fear of death moves inside me.

HYWEL chanted Meirionnydd's charm –
His pillow was a girl's white arm.
Now he is whiter far than she.
The fear of death is inside me.

PRYDYDD y MOCH would smile to see
An Englishman – if he was maggoty
Now he is grinning bonily.
The fear of death moves inside me.

DAFYDD ap GWILYM did women much good
At the cuckoo's church in the green wood.
Death ended his sweet ministry.
The fear of death moves inside me.

GWERFYL MECHAIN wrote in cheerful tones
Of the human body's tropical zones.

She shared DAFYDD's hot philosophy.
The fear of death moves inside me.

IOLO GOCH wrote of any old thing –
Girls, feasts and even an English King.
They say he died most professionally.
The fear of death moves inside me.

GRUFFUDD GRYG wept desperately
For the North of Wales in her poverty.
He was a bird from heaven's country –
The fear of death moves inside me.

LLYWELYN GOCH's fist dared to knock
On the heavy door with the black steel lock.
A skull told him its history.
The fear of death is inside me.

SION CENT, who sang thank you to his purse,
RHYS GOCH, who killed a fox with verse,
Sleep in the gravel dormitory –
The fear of death moves inside me.

IEUAN ap RHYDDERCH so scholarly
GWERFUL MADOG of famed hospitality,
LEWYS GLYN COTHI who loved luxury –
The fear of death moves inside me.

DAFYDD ap EDMWND's singing skill
Thrilled through all Wales. Then it fell still.
LEWIS MON wrote his elegy.
The fear of death moves inside me.

BEDO BRWNLLYS, IEUAN DEULWYN,
GUTYN OWAIN, TUDUR PENLLYN,
All exiles in Death's monarchy.
The fear of death moves inside me.

Life was dark-coloured to TUDUR ALED.
WILLIAM LLYN brooded on the dead.
SION TUDUR mocked all vanity.
The fear of death moves inside me.

DIC HUWS dedicated a roundelay
To a girl by the name of Break of Day.
Night broke on both of them, remorselessly –
The fear of death moves inside me.

And hundreds have since joined the towering choir –
Poets of Wales, like trees on fire,
Light the black twentieth century.
The fear of death moves inside me.

Oh DYLAN THOMAS, as bright as nails,
Could make no kind of living in Wales
So he died of American charity –
The fear of death moves inside me.

Terror of death, terror of death,
Terror of death, terror of death,
That drumbeat sounds relentlessly.
The fear of death moves inside me.

Since we must all of us ride down
The black hill into the black town,
Let us sing out courageously.
The fear of death moves inside me.

The black lungs swell, the black harp sighs,
Whenever a Welsh maker dies.
Forgive my nervous balladry.
Timor mortis conturbat me.

THE OWL SONG

I have walked through the valley of slate
And the rain was blue
I have seen the sky like a hunter's net
Deepest darkest blue
I have seen the bit tight in the horse's teeth
And the bit was blue
I have heard the swords sing on the battlefield
And the swords were blue
I have seen the eyes of my dead enemy
They were round as the face of my friend in the dawn
On the sheep-shorn grass – his face was blue

Blue
Grave
Blue
Gravel on a grave
Blue
Flowers on the gravel on a grave

And I shall wake in the blue night
And sleep in the blue day
And I will live my own blue life
In the blue tree, in the blue tree

And my food shall be blue
And my wine shall be blue
And my mind shall be filled
With nothing but blue

blue blue   blue blue   blue blue

ASTERIX AND THE GREAT DIVIDE

I'm a long-term fan of both Ken Campbell and the Unicorn
Theatre. So these were fun to write for Ken's Asterix
adaptation. I believe they were criticised for glorifying
drunkenness, matrimony and violence, not necessarily in
that order.

Composer: ILONA SEKACZ.

Performed: Unicorn Theatre for Children.

176

WEDDING SONG

Play the merry organ
Clang the bells
Pass me a gallon of wine.
Congratulate the bridegrooms
Kiss the bride
Isn't it time to dine?
With a ding dong ding dong
Gilly gilly gong
And a Gaul with a ging gong goo.

Marriage is a very solemn ceremony
Entered into for the future's sake
Marriage is a very solemn ceremony
Aren't they ever going to slice the cake?

Congratulate the organ
Kiss the bells
Pass me a gallon of wine.
Play the merry bridegroom
Clang the bride
Isn't it time to dine?
With a ding dong ding dong
Gilly gilly gong
And a Gaul with a ging gong goo!

OBELIX SONG

I love to brawl
Cos I'm a Gaul
All dressed up to conquer
If I meet
A Roman in the street
I biff him on the honker

ROMAN MARCHING SONG

Romans . . . Romans . . .
Wishing we were home
Hic Haec Hoc
We love to rock
Around the Hippodrome
Romans . . . Romans . . .
Roaming far from home
Veni vidi vici
Don't you be so cheeky
All roads lead to Rome.

GAUL'S SONG

Some villains vow by the Vikings
Some hail the hairy Huns
But they're not to our likings
For the Gauls are the mighty ones
Oh yes
The Gauls are the mighty ones

Well the Gods love a Gaul
And the Gauls love a Gaul
Gauls Rule OK to the end
But you'll never catch
The Gaul of the Match
Cos diamonds are a Gaul's best friend.

Beggars may bow to the Briton
Curs may kow-tow to the Celts
Nits bend their knees to the Nipponese
But the Gauls are something else
Oh yes
The Gauls are something else

Well the Gods love a Gaul
And the Gauls love a Gaul
Gauls rule OK to the end
But you'll never catch
The Gaul of the Match
Cos diamonds are a Gaul's best friend

A CHILD'S CHRISTMAS IN WALES

My friend Jeremy Brooks, novelist, poet and adapter of Russian stage classics, asked me to collaborate on this project because of my experience of making plays with songs (as opposed to "talking plays" as they get called in my family).

I was very happy to, because I love Dylan Thomas and believe that he's currently underestimated. Particularly his very popular radio pieces, in which he found a kind of poetry which could reach an audience as large as Dickens.

Christmas was always a very happy time in my childhood — as it still is, a time with its own rituals and family memories and the same old jokes and cracker mottoes. Jeremy lives in Wales much of the time, but neither of us knew Swansea well. So we went down to explore. Our guide was the poet Nigel Jenkins, who lives in Mumbles and was able to show us all Dylan's old haunts. We spent most time in Cwmdonkin Park and on the seashore, which were to feature in the play later as the two outdoor scenes, taking notes and photos.

We divided the play into sections and each took about half of them, later making rewrite suggestions to each other. *A Child's Christmas In Wales* was of course the backbone of the show, and we followed the boy Dylan from Christmas Eve to Christmas evening, inserting a few Dylanish incidents from other works, our own memories and inventions and some new lyrics to old tunes.

It was conceived as a family show and that's how it works best, especially when the audience is full of three generations.

180

Composer: all traditional tunes.

Performed: Great Lakes Festival, Cleveland, 1983 and
1984. Since then in Milford Haven, Mold,
Harrogate, Dublin etc.

THE SOFT SNOW FALLS ALL AROUND

(to the tune of *The Green Grass Grows All Around*)

Now in the world
There lay a land
The prettiest land
That you ever did see
                The land of Wales

O the land in the world
And the world in the sky
And the soft snow falls all around
All around
The soft snow falls all around

And in that land
There sleeps a town
The prettiest town
That you ever did see
              Swansea

O the town in the land
And the land in the world
And the world in the sky
And the soft snow falls all around
All around
The soft snow falls all around

And in that town
Was built a house
The prettiest house
That you ever did see
              Semi-detached

O the house in the town
And the town in the land
And the land in the world
And the world in the sky

And the soft snow falls all around
All around
The soft snow falls all around

And in that house
There was a bed
The prettiest bed
That you ever did see

O the bed in the house
And the house in the town
And the town in the land
And the land in the world
And the world in the sky
And the soft snow falls all around
All around
The soft snow falls all around.

And in that bed
There was a boy
The prettiest boy
That you ever did see
      Tough as toffee

O the boy in the bed
And the bed in the house
And the house in the town
And the town in the land
And the land in the world
And the world in the sky
And the soft snow falls all around
All around
The soft snow falls all around

OH, CHRISTMAS MEANS PUDDING

(to the tune of *Llwyn On/The Ash Grove*)

Oh, Christmas means pudding
And pudding means Christmas
A pudding of glory, with brandy ablaze
The darkest of puddings
The brightest of puddings
A pudding to light us
Through winter's dark days

There's good in the pudding
There's apples and lemons
Sultanas and breadcrumbs, chopped suet and rum
There's candied peel, almonds, eggs,
Flour, spice and sugar,
There's good in the pudding
Oh, please slice me some!

SHINING HEART

(to the tune of *Calon Lan*)

Shining heart is full of goodness
Purer than the lily's white
Shining heart is always singing
All the day and all the night

Do not give me golden money
Or the stones from diamond mines
For I want a heart that's happy,
Honest heart, a heart that shines
Jewels glitter for a moment

Then are lost in endless night
But the pure and perfect heart shines
With a warm eternal light

Shining heart is full of goodness
Purer than the lily's white
Shining heart is always shining
All the day and all the night

THE TELL-A-TALE SONG

(to the tune of *O Come, O Come, Emmanuel*)

O tell a tale of something terrible
And make it really ho-o-orrible
About a boy who found a head
And armies of the living dead

O tell a tale of something terrible
And make it really ho-o-orrible

O tell a tale to set us shivering
About a mermaid's poi-oi-oisoned ring
And grisly details of a curse
And how the devil wooed a nurse

O tell a tale of something terrible
And make it really ho-o-orrible

O tell a tale a truly dreadful yarn
About a heap of jelly in a barn
And bats that have a human brain
And serpents coming up the drain

O tell a tale of something terrible
And make it really ho-o-orrible
O tell a tale to feed our nightmares on
Of that black country where the dead have gone

And babies boiled up into broth
To feed the ghost of a gigantic moth

O tell a tale of something terrible
And make it really ho-o-orrible

RAISING THE TITANIC

Welfare State International asked me to work on this amazing show, which they staged in London docks, but I was very short of time. All I could do was travel to their Ulverston headquarters and hold some song workshops for the cast. The idea was that each person should write a song for their own character, helped by a small team of composers.

This went well, but I did find time to write a few lyrics for that adventure.

Composer: LUK MISHALLE.

Performed: London, 1984.

SHE'S FINE FINE FINE

She's fine fine fine
They call her the Titanic
Of the White Star Line
She's fine fine fine
They call her the Titanic
Of the White Star Line

She weigh
Sixty thousand
Sixty six thousand ton

She got
Fifty thousand horse power

And she's fine fine fine
They call her the Titanic
Of the White Star Line
She's fine fine fine
They call her the Titanic
Of the White Star Line

She make
Twenty four twenty five knots an hour
Twenty four twenty five knots an hour
And she's shoving black smoke at the overhead sun
Shoving black smoke at the overhead sun

And she's fine fine fine
They call her the Titanic
Of the White Star Line
She's fine fine fine
They call her the Titanic
Of the White Star Line

She got
Sixty foot funnels
Three million rivets

Everything the human race could afford
Everything the human race could afford

And she's fine fine fine
They call her the Titanic
Of the White Star Line
She's fine fine fine
They call her the Titanic
Of the White Star Line

She got
Two thousand two hundred and seven people on board
Two thousand two hundred and seven people on board

And she's fine fine fine
They call her the titanic
of the White Star Line
She's fine fine fine
They call her the Titanic
Of the White Star Line

UNTHINKABLE SONG

Don't think the unthinkable
Dance to the ragtime band
How could they sink the unsinkable?
Trust in the captain's hand.
Let's drink what is drinkable.
Nobody's going to drown.
How could they sink the unsinkable?
How could the world burn down?

THE MENU

Choicest oysters
Fresh on the ice
Olga Consommé
Not so keen
Cream of Barley
Sounds pretty nice
Then I'll try Salmon
With Sauce Mousseline

    Bring me a Bourbon
    Pour me a Port
    Fire off the best Champagne
    Try the bouquet of this Beaujolais
    Let's have Champagne again

Whatever you fancy
Whatever you crave
If you cry out for the moon
You shall eat the full moon
With a silver spoon
In the first class dining saloon

Filet Mignons
Could be quite good
Sauté of Chicken
Lyonnaise
Marrow Farcie
Leave room for your pud
Have to watch my figure
Nowadays

    Bring me a Brandy
    Slosh me a Scotch
    Pop me the best Champagne
    Pass the Bordeaux, let the Chablis flow
    Make it Champagne again

Whatever you fancy
Whatever you crave
If you cry out for the moon
You shall eat the full moon
With a silver spoon
In the first class dining saloon

Lamb and mint Sauce
Followed by Duck
Chateau Potatoes
Roast Beef
Pass the Creamed Carrots
What's this muck?
That's boiled rice.
It's beyond belief.

> Shteward a Sherry
> Armagnac here
> Champagne improves the brain
> No that's all hooey make mine Drambuie
> Why not Champagne again?

Whatever you fancy
Whatever you crave
If you cry out for the moon
You shall eat the full moon
With a Silver spoon
In the first class dining saloon

Cold Asparagus
Vinaigrette
Pâté de Foie Gras
Squab and Cress
This is one meal
That I won't forget
The duchess's dress
Could hardly be less

> Waiter! Some alcohol
> Make it quick
> Champagne? Is this champagne?

Jesus my lover's being sick
Bring him champagne again

Whatever you fancy
Whatever you crave
If you cry out for the moon
You shall eat the full moon
With a silver spoon
In the first class dining saloon

Waldorf Pudding
Chocolate eclairs
Peaches in jelly
Chartreuse
What do you think of
Vickers shares?
Mainly depends if
A war occurs

Drink me a pour please
Any old booze
Champagne – are you Pam Shane?
Let's drink a toast to a super cruise
Champagne! Must be champagne!

Whatever you fancy
Whatever you crave
If you cry out for the moon
You shall eat the full moon
With a silver spoon
Last sitting
Last sitting
In the first class dining saloon . . .

192

THE TRAGEDY OF KING REAL

A version of *King Lear* set at the beginning of a nuclear war. This was written for Welfare State International, who decided to make it into a movie.

It's not in any sense a send-up of *King Lear*, which I love above all plays. It borrows shamelessly from Shakespeare and tries to discover why it is that some people can contemplate the ending of life on earth as a possible choice.

Composer: PETE MOSER.

Filmed: As *King Real And The Hoodlums* by Welfare State International, 1984.

Published: In *Peace Plays – 1* edited by Stephen Lowe, Methuen, 1985.

I SAW A VISION

I saw a vision on my vision machine
I saw a vision but what did it mean?
Vision of puppets playing power games
Vision of the world like a flower in flames
Pain of the planet beating in my head
Pain of the planet till the planet went dead.
I saw a vision on my vision machine
I saw a vision but what did it mean?
I wish I knew
I wish I knew
I wish I knew.

KING REAL

King Real
Rules the land and the sea.
King Real
To the power of three.
King Real King Real
You'd better get your knees in training to kneel
And practise crawling on your belly like an eel
Or he'll run you over in his Royalmobile
King Real – that real King – King Real

King Real
All victorious
King Real
Ultra-glorious
King Real King Real
When he marches into battle hear his enemies squeal

For he smashes them and bashes them from head
        to heel
With cast-iron clobberers and slicers of steel
King Real – that real King – King Real.

King Real
Real as real estate
King Real King Real
Real
As the wheel of fate
King Real King Real
He generously tells us what to think and feel
For a king must be king like a bell has to peal
And he knows the common man's a bloody imbecile
King Real – that real real real real real real King –
        King Real!

GONILLA'S SONG

My love breeds in the tropical heat
Hanging upside down from palm trees by its feet
My love's mango and my love's peaches
And a million crawling and coiling creatures
My love's an everglades alligator
And it hugs the world round the equator
        And when my love beats
        It goes bompety-bomp
        My love's doing
        The stomp in the swamp

Rainforest fever and breadfruit pie
My love's brighter than the sun in your eye
My love's simple as a bunch of bananas
Funky as a monkey that swings on lianas

And if all that loving doesn't win me one key
Daddy, you've made a monkey out of me.
> And when my love beats
> It goes bompety-bomp
> My love's doing
> The stomp in the swamp.

THE DANCE OF THE KEYS

The dance of the keys
Is the dance of one
The silver of swords
And the silver gun

And the dance of one
Is a dance of stone
And the dance of one
Must be danced alone

And the time of the dance
It is zero hour
And the dance of the keys
Is the dance of power

The dance of the keys
Is the dance of two
The rhythm of gold
Swaying me and you

And the dance of two
Is a dance of tears
And the dance of two
Must be danced in pairs

And the time of the dance
It is zero hour

196

And the dance of the keys
Is the dance of power

The dance of the keys
Is the dance of three
The music of pain
And of destiny.

And the dance of three
As they skip and hop
Is the dance for three
That must never stop

And the time of the dance
It is zero hour
And the dance of the keys
Is the dance of power.

CLAUDELLA'S SONG

O no, I never loved you best of all
O no, I could not love you properly
For you controlled the ways
In which I spent my days
And you could order me to laugh or cry
And you could order me to live or die
Because I was your royal property
Because I was your royal property.

You were Father Christmas
And I longed for you
You were the hangman
And I hid from you
You were the ice-cream man
I worshipped you

You were the scissorman
I dreamed of you
How could I love you
When I always knew
I was the unicorn
In your concrete zoo?

And so I never loved you best of all
O no, I could not love you properly
Because you would not let me love you properly.

PARTY GAMES

Hunt the blister
Who Gets the Goose?
Banana Dancing
Musical Noose
Or – imitate your favourite river.

Pass the Finger
Juggling with rats
Tricks with crutches
Sterilising bats
Or – imitate your favourite window.

Sur le pont
D'Avignon
Water's boiling water's boiling

Treacle Swinging
Suck the Rag
Who's In the Big Black
Polythene Bag?
Or – imitate your favourite currency.

May sound funny

198

But these are the names
Of some of the brave new
Party games.

Lemon Swapping
Ripping Rippings
Build a cathedral
From your Toenail Clippings
Or – imitate your favourite plague.

Ant Embalming
Rape the Clown
Agatha Christie's
Upside Down
Or – imitate your favourite archipelago.

Parents and children have I none
But I have a shelter and I have a gun.

ADDERMAN'S SONG

My mother was a desert
My father was a bone
And I was born
To burn the world to stone.

I went to school at Nightmare
They taught me how to fear
I want to slit the human race
From ear to ugly ear.

Cos I'm crazy 'bout nothing
Gotta have that good nothing
Gimme my sweet nothing
Nothing nothing.

Working in a factory
Smoke and slamming steel
Sucking on the valium
Until I couldn't feel.

Found myself redundant
Buggered off to rot
Came back pleading for a job
Nothing's what I got.

Now I'm crazy 'bout nothing
Gotta have that good nothing
Gimme sweet nothing
Nothing nothing.

Joined the British Army
Learned a steady trade
British Army showed me
How nothing is made

And now

Nothing is my woman
We live in Nothing Town
On a nothing planet
That we just burned down.

Cos we're crazy 'bout nothing
Gotta have that nothing
Gimme sweet nothing
Nothing nothing

C'MON EVERYBODY

A show of my songs and poems performed by Pete Moser, my daughter Sasha Mitchell and myself, produced by David Jones. The young artist Jenni Gregory designed some amazing background screens for us depicting *The Jungle of Eden*. (Which I still use for shows whenever possible.) She also designed our costumes.

It was a happy show and we had good crowds and smashing reviews on tour and in London.

Composer: PETE MOSER.

Performed: On tour in England and Scotland and Tricycle Theatre, 1984.

THE TRUTH

The truth is the truth
Is a strange kind of animal
The truth is the truth
Only comes out when people sleep
So I stay awake listening for the truth

> The truth's my favourite uncle
> Always brings me a surprise
> The truth's my favourite uncle
> What ridiculous stories it tells

I like the truth I like the way it doesn't simper
I like the truth it employs no PR men
I like the truth I'm very fond of its music
I like the truth I like the way it tastes
I like the truth it never gazes into mirrors
I like the truth I like its way of walking
I like the truth I'm very fond of its music
I like the truth I enjoy the way it tastes
I really love the truth

If it licks me I know it wants to lick me
If it leaves me I know it must be on its way

For the truth is the truth
Is a strange kind of animal
The truth is the truth
Only comes out when people sleep
So I stay awake listening for the truth

> It doesn't make hit records
> It's not often on the TV
> You'll see the truth more often
> In the sadness of faces on trains

I like its grin I like its way of falling silent
I like the way that it snoozes on committees
At soccer games it watches how the grass grows

It rents a shop and puts the worst in the window
I saw the truth in a junkyard one evening
I saw the truth it was sitting by a bonfire
I asked the truth, I said: What's your kind of music?
Tell you the truth, said truth, I like shining music
Yes I love the truth

For the truth is the truth
Is a strange kind of animal
The truth is the truth
Only comes out when people sleep
So I stay awake listening for the truth
Yes I stay awake listening for the truth

ODE TO HER

You so draggy Ms Maggie
The way you drag us down
The way you shake your finger
The way you frown your frown
But a day's soon dawning
When all the world will shout
We gonna catch yer Ms Thatcher
You'll be dragged out

You so draggy Ms Maggie
You tore this land apart
With your smile like a laser
And your iceberg heart
You taught the old and jobless
What poverty means
You sent the young men killing
Irish and the Argentines

You so draggy Ms Maggie
With your million cuts
You slashed this country
Till it spilled its guts
You crucified parents
And their children too
Nailed em up by the million
Here's what we'll do

You so draggy Ms Maggie
Madonna of the rich
We gonna introduce you
On the Anfield pitch
Oh you can talk your meanest
But you're as good as dead
When Yosser Hughes butts you
With his poor old head . . .

NEW SKIPPING RHYMES

Good little Georgie
Worked like a madman
Three years at Oxford
Five years an adman
Went on Mastermind
Did so well on that show
Now he's the host
Of a TV Chat Show

> My savings are my baby
> Money is my boss
> My mummy and my daddy
> Were profit and loss
> One thousand, two thousand, three
> thousand, four. . . .

Meat on the hook
Powder in the jar
Mickey Jagger is a Star
S-T-A-R spells Star
He can whistle
He can hum
He can wriggle his umpumbum

> Pretty little Pam
> Passed her exam
> What shall we give her?
> Doughnuts and jam
>
> Stupid little Sam
> Failed his exam
> What shall we give him?
> Who gives a damn?

FIFTEEN MILLION PLASTIC BAGS

I was walking in a government warehouse
Where the daylight never goes
I saw fifteen million plastic bags
Hanging in a thousand rows

And five million bags were six feet long
Five million were five foot five
Five million were stamped with Mickey Mouse
And they came in a smaller size

Were they for guns or uniforms
Or a dirty kind of party game?
Then I saw each bag had a number
And every bag bore a name.
And five million bags were six feet long
Five million were five foot five

Five million were stamped with Mickey Mouse
And they came in a smaller size

So I've taken my bag from the hanger
And I've pulled it over my head
And I'll wait for the priest to zip it
So the radiation won't spread.

Now five million bags are six feet long
Five million are five foot five
Five million are stamped with Mickey Mouse
And they come in a smaller size . . .

I was walking in a government warehouse
Where the daylight never goes
I saw fifteen million plastic bags
Hanging in a thousand rows

ANIMAL FARM

When Peter Hall asked me to write four or five lyrics for his adaptation of Orwell's "fairy tale" he must have known that I'd produce about 26 lyrics. He made room for most of them. And he asked who I'd like as composer, so I asked for Dick Peaslee, whom I hadn't worked with since *US*.

Of the lyrics here, *Sugarcandy Mountain* is sung by the preaching crow, *Twenty-Seven Ribbons* is the song of Molly the pony who leaves the Revolution for the comforts of free enterprise, *Boulder Song* is a song of solidarity among comrade animals, *Nothing Song* is about how to survive in a totalitarian state, and *The Runt of the Litter* is a number in which Napoleon explains his rise to power – something Orwell doesn't go into, but which seemed necessary on stage. *I See The Future* was another departure from or extension of Orwell, in which I attempted to show both Eastern and Western governments of today enchanted by the idea of running their countries like profitable battery farms. I don't think Orwell would have objected to the idea, but the song never worked properly. I'd written very concentrated lyrics, which can only be understood if delivered slowly, but the dramatic placing of the song called for a fast tempo. But I still believe the words are worth a glance.

Personally I didn't want the actors to wear masks and go on crutches, but once the decision had been made I shut up about it. I do believe that everyone working on a show has the right to comment on every aspect of the show. My own method is to go home and type out a memo to the

207

director including any thoughts I have about the show. A memo is best because then (a) the director can read it in his or her own time and (b) you've both got a record of suggestions which can then be ticked or crossed off.

Some friends on the Left looked somewhat stony when they heard I was involved with *Animal Farm*. So it goes.

I'd first read the book when I was about ten. I'd been given it by my new teacher, Michael Bell, who'd asked me what I liked reading about. I said "imaginary countries" and he gave me *Animal Farm* and Samuel Butler's *Erewhon*. I understood and loved Orwell's story, although I didn't connect it with human politics. Today I see the book as a socialist critique of the Soviet revolution, undermined by its fear of majority decisions and by its creation of a new ruling class. The book has certainly been used as Cold War propaganda. A Turkish friend told me that in his prison cell he was only allowed the Koran and *Animal Farm*. Part of the reason why I wanted to be involved in the production was that the story can easily be twisted into anti-socialist propaganda. I think Peter Hall's production avoided that trap and was a warning to all revolutionaries – "Watch out for the pigs".

Composer: RICHARD PEASLEE.

Performed: National Theatre, 1984.

SUGARCANDY MOUNTAIN

Beyond the fences of this Life
There lies a wondrous hill
And all good creatures when they die
Go there to graze their fill.

On Sugarcandy Mountain
No labouring is done.
Beside a milky fountain
The beasts lie in the sun.
On Sugarcandy Mountain
You'll find Black Treacle Lake,
Lump sugar beyond counting
And fields of linseed cake.

So fear no more the knacker's yard,
Nor dread the abattoir,
But work today so you may join
That Sugarcandy choir.

On Sugarcandy Mountain
We'll find Black Treacle Lake
Lump sugar beyond counting
And fields of linseed cake.

TWENTY-SEVEN RIBBONS

The wheels flow around
With a whirring, purring sound
As I step along Speedwell Lane,
And I hurry home
To the curry-comb
With twenty-seven multi-coloured ribbons in my mane.

Twenty-seven ribbons
Sugar lumps for Mollie
A kindly blacksmith
And a gentle vet.
Master bought my ribbons
And my shiny brasses –
Give the humans what they want
And that is what you'll get.

And the wheels flow around
With a whirring, purring sound
As I step along Speedwell Lane,
And I hurry home
To the curry-comb
With twenty-seven multi-coloured ribbons in my mane.

Twenty-seven ribbons,
Sugar lumps for Mollie
A careful grooming
After every trip.
I have heard some horses
Say that man is cruel –
But if you're obedient
You'll seldom feel the whip.

Yes the wheels flow around
With a whirring, purring sound
As I step along Speedwell Lane,
And I hurry home
To the curry-comb
With twenty-seven multi-coloured ribbons in my mane.
Twenty-seven ribbons,
Twenty-seven ribbons,
Twenty-seven ribbons in my mane.

BOULDER SONG

BOXER:
> There was a whacking great
> limestone boulder
>> Must have weighed near a
> ton.
> I tried to shift it with me shoulder
> –
>> – Couldn't be done.
>
> So I called a passing comrade over
>> And she came at the run.

BOXER AND CLOVER:
> We tried to move that limestone
> boulder –
>> – Couldn't be done.
>
> We appealed to the Sheep
> Committee
>> Called up the Goats' Brigade
> And the chickens and the geese to
> shift that rock –

ALL ANIMALS:
>> – But it just stayed.
>
> It just stayed where it was
> That great lump of stone
> And all of the beasts
> Gave a mighty moan.

A SHEEP:
> We'll never shift it!

A HEN:
> The rock's too big!

SQUEALER:
> Give it one more try,
> Says a stout-hearted pig!

ALL ANIMALS:
> So we gave one more shove
> And we gave one more lift
> And that whacking great boulder
> Started to shift

And we gave it a shove
With all our heart and soul
And that whacking great boulder
Started to roll – and roll – and roll
and – (CRASH!)

There was a whacking great
limestone boulder
   But animals worked as one
Yes, through animal cooperation
   Anything can be done!

THE GREEN FLAG

Our land was once a forest
All green from shore to shore,
Till humans tore the greenwood down
With axe and fire and saw.

   But see! The banners of the grass are raised!
   The trees are striding through the dawn!
   And the Green Flag is flying
   With the signs of Hoof and Horn.
   Yes, Man is fleeing from the countryside
   And soon our meadows shall be clean,
   For the Green Flag is flying
   And all England shall be green.

REVISED AND IMPROVED VERSION OF THE GREEN
FLAG CHORUS by MINIMUS

   But see! The trotters of the pigs are raised!
   The swine advance with bellies stout!
   And the Green Flag is flying
   With the Curly Tail and Snout!

Yes, pigs are leading all the animals.
Oh, follow them, nor reason why,
For the Green Flag is flying
And all England is our Stye.

NOTHING SONG

Say what you think
But the best thing to think
Is nothing –
That's excellent thinking.

Eat what you like
But the best food to like
Is nothing –
It's not on the ration.

Do what you want
But the best place to go
Is nowhere –
You might get permission.

Obey them.
When they tell you what to do.
You are nothing
Nothing.

Believe them
When they tell you what is true.
You are nothing.
Nothing.

Keep your nose to the grindstone
And your shoulder to the wheel.
Listen
When they tell you what to feel
And –

Feel what you like
But the best thing to feel
Is nothing

Nothing.

THE RUNT OF THE LITTER

On the dusty day when I was born
I was not very big.
In fact, of a litter of seventeen,
I was the smallest pig.
It was more of a scramble than a birthday
And I came out back to front.
I was the last of the bunch
When it came to lunch.
Yes, I was the litter's runt.

But a runt has to fight
For his share of the milk
If he fancies staying alive.
He'll kick out with his feet
And cling on to that teat
And the runt may yet survive.

And if that young runt
Grabs enough of the swill
Then his bite will be worse than his grunt.
He'll grow stately and stout
With an elegant snout
But he knows he was the runt.

And the runt seizes power
For he knows all the tricks –
Those he bites will never bite back.
And the piglet who once

Was the weakest of runts
Shall be the leader of the pack.

I SEE THE FUTURE

Manor Farm!

Manor Farm!

More profit for fewer people!

More power in fewer hands!

More control of beast and human!

Use every inch of the land!

I see the future
Shine on me
And pictures
Of the times to be –

Where chickens hatch
Ten thousand eggs
And never need
To stretch their legs.

And sheep in crates
May spend their days
And grow us wool
But never graze.

The silky mink,
The fiery fox,
Shall grow us fur
Inside a box.

And calves be born,
Grow up, give birth,
And die but never
Walk on earth.

I see the future
Shine on me
And pictures
Of the times to be,
Where day and night
And heat and cold
And birth and death
Are all controlled
And profit rules
And all is calm
On England's grey
And modern farm.

GREENHAM COMMON

I was asked by a woman friend to write some songs to be
sung at the Greenham demonstrations against nuclear
murder. I concentrated on new versions of Beatles tunes.
Not the most subtle lyrics in the world, but they're
singable.

Composer: LENNON/MCCARTNEY.

Performed: Outside Greenham, 1985.

POWER TO THE PEOPLE

Power to the people
Power to the people
Power to the people right on

You say you want a peaceful planet
We'd better get it on right away
Well get down to the camp
Down in the damp
Singing

Power to the people
Power to the people
Power to the people right on

A million women demonstrating
You'd better give us what we really want
And the USAF
Better stop playing deaf
When we sing

Power to the people
Power to the people
Power to the people
Power to the people
Power to the people right on

I'm gonna ask you coppers and airmen
How much you love your children back home.
They need peace you know if they are going to grow
And they'll sing

Power to the people
Power to the people
Power to the people
Power to the people right on

KILLER SUBMARINE

In the town where I was born
Lived a man who served the Queen
And he told me of his work
In a killer submarine

With their rockets aimed to wipe
Prague and Moscow from the scene
They patrol beneath the waves
In their killer submarines

They all live in a killer submarine
Killer submarine, killer submarine
They all live in a killer submarine
Killer submarine, killer submarine

And the Soviets as well
Have a submarine next door
and the band begins to play

They all live in a killer submarine
Killer submarine, killer submarine
They all live in a killer submarine
Killer submarine, killer submarine

And they live a life of fear
In their murderous and mad machines
Captain Lunacy's in charge
Of their killer submarines

They'll all die in their killer submarines
Killer submarines, killer submarines
They'll all die in their killer submarines
Killer submarines, killer submarines

A HARD DAY'S NIGHT

It's been a hard day's night
And I've been living in a bog
It's been a hard day's night
I should be sleeping like a log
But I'm seeing it through
Because of things that they do
Upon this murder site

You know I'm here all day
Demonstrating along with you
And it's worth it just to hear them say
That they don't know what to do
So why on earth should I stop
When every airman and cop
Knows we're gonna get our way

Now we're here and we'll make everything right
Now we're here, we can unite in our fight, right, yeh

It's been a hard day's night
And I've been living in a bog
It's been a hard day's night
I should be sleeping like a log
But I'm seeing it through
Because of things that they do
Upon this murder site

So why on earth should I stop
When every airman and cop
Knows we're gonna get our way

A LITTLE HELP FROM OUR FRIENDS

What would you do if I closed down our base?
Would you fire silver bullets at me?
Lend me your ears and I'll sing you a song
And you'll walk out and link arms with me.
I'll ban Cruise with a little help from my friends
I'll do more with a little help from my friends
I'll stop war with a little help from my friends

What do I do with my family away?
Doesn't worry me I'm not alone.
How do I feel at the end of the day?
I'm shagged out but I'm not on my own.
No, I get by with a little help from my friends,
I get high with a little help from my friends
Oh I'm gonna try with a little help from my friends.

Are there more women needed?
The world needs plenty of love.
Can it be any woman?
The world needs all of our love.

Would you believe in a peace that will last?
Yes I'm certain that we'll make it stick this time.
What does it look like, this peace that will last?
I can't tell you but I know it's mine
We'll ban Cruise with a little help from our friends
We'll do more with a little help from our friends
We'll stop war with a little help from our friends

Are there more women needed?
The world needs plenty of love
Can it be any woman?
The world needs all of our love
Oh we'll ban Cruise with a little help from our friends
We'll close the base with a little help from our friends
We'll do more with a little help from our friends

We'll stop war with a little help from our friends
With a little help from our friends

PICKET FOR PEACE

I think we're gonna stop Cruise
We'll stop it today
The missile they'll never use
Is going away

We got a picket for peace
We got a picket for pea-ea-eace
We got a picket for peace
And we will win

We say that nuclear war
Could burn the world down, yeah,
We will never be free
While war is around

We got a picket for peace
We got a picket for pea-ea-eace
We got a picket for peace
And we will win

I don't know what's in parliament's head
They ought to think twice
They ought to do right by us
Before they get to waking up dead
They ought to do right by us

I think we're gonna stop Cruise
We'll stop it today
The missile they'll never use
Is going away

We got a picket for peace
We got a picket for peace
We got a picket for peace
And we will win

Yes we gonna win
Yes we gonna win

ON THE LOOSE

A touring cabaret show headed by Pete Moser of Welfare State International. I spent a week in Ulverston working with the cast. They were basically musicians and singers but we had the idea that people would like an evening in which musicians not only play but tell, through songs, sketches or direct speech, stories from their own lives. We invented a framework about a guy in search of people to form a band.

My main job in that week was to encourage people to make their own songs. We started telling stories about our own lives. Some stories were funny, some sad, many now forgotten, but some of them became songs. The two included here were both inspired by the Zulu singer and dancer Doreen Webster.

Blue Cotton was based on a true story which Doreen told us. *Angel Water* came about because I'd seen, in an earlier Welfare State show, a moving papier maché skeleton of a baby. When Doreen acted this song the baby was kept wrapped in a shawl and it was only in the last verse that the audience realised that the baby had been stripped to its skeleton by Famine. The mother herself did not realise it, but kept nursing her baby.

The tune of *Angel Water* is slow and mournful and is designed to include elaborate costumes and, between the penultimate and last verse, a dancing contest, in which the woman dances Famine and his two assistants into the ground and so wins back her baby.

Composer: PETE MOSER and BORIS HOWARTH (*Blues and Kisses*)

Performed: On tour 1986 and 1987.

Blues and Kisses in fact was made for another Welfare State show – *Tales For A Winter Night* (1976) – about which I don't know enough to warrant a section.

ANGEL WATER

(A woman enters)

There was a woman and she could not have a baby
There was a woman and she could not have a baby
Tried and tried but she could not have a baby
And she cried in the shadows her soul

She had a dream about an angel in the river
She had a dream about an angel in the river
A golden angel sleeping in the river
So she walked to the muddy waterside

And she looked
Deep
Down into the river
And she saw
Her
Angel's golden eyes
And she dived
Deep
Down into the river
And she made
Love
Till the mighty river ran dry

(She takes a bundle containing a baby)

She had a baby and she called her Angel Water
She had a baby and she called her Angel Water
A laughing baby and she called her Angel Water
And she told her the stories of her soul

(Famine appears)

One burning day there was a traveller in her doorway
His hands were thorny, his hands were full of ashes
His face was empty and his voice was like a desert
And he called Angel Water by her name

He said My name is Famine and I've come here on
     a mission
He said My name is Famine and I've come to take your
     baby
He said My name is Famine and I've come for Angel Water
You must place Angel Water in my arms

And she looked
Deep
In the eyes of Famine
And she said
No
Angel Water's mine
And she heard
His
Angry hungry laughter
But she held
Tight
To her warm and wonderful child

He took the baby down the dry and dusty river
He took the baby down a dry and dusty tunnel
He took the baby through the dry and dusty darkness
To his dry, dusty palace underground.

(A diamond lady and a smiling soldier appear)

The woman followed but the palace gate was guarded
A diamond lady with a diamond pistol
A smiling soldier with a dagger on each finger
And they bowed down to Famine as their King

Surrender woman, you can never conquer Famine
Yes I surrender, Famine, but on one condition –
I want to dance with you, and with your diamond woman
And with your smiling soldier underground.

(She dances against each of them. She dances all three into
     the ground. She takes back her baby. It is a
     skeleton now, but she does not realise.)

There is a woman and she wanders with her baby
There is a woman and she wanders with her baby
There is a woman and she wanders with her baby
And she sings her the stories of her soul.

BLUE COTTON

Blue cotton
Blue cotton

She wore a blue cotton dress
With a pattern of flowers
A blue cotton dress
With a pattern of flowers
Blue cotton dress
With a pattern of a hundred flowers

> She appeared at the crossroads
> With a clipboard in her hand
> She stepped into the highway
> And she raised up her hand
> And my Fiat just managed
> A spectacular emergency stop
>
> So I yelled at the woman:
> Get the hell off the road
> Or else you're going to find you're
> Being squashed like a toad
> But she wrote down my number
> As if she was some kind of cop

She wore a blue cotton dress
With a pattern of flowers
A blue cotton dress
With a pattern of flowers

Blue cotton dress
With a pattern of a hundred flowers

Well I parked at the corner
And watched from afar
And driver after driver
Had to pull up his car
And she wrote down their numbers
And dismissed them with a wave of her hand.

And she stands at the crossroads
Every empty day to wait
Recording every number
On each numberplate
In her search for the number
Of the driver who ran over her man

She wore a blue cotton dress
With a pattern of flowers
A blue cotton dress
With a pattern of flowers
Blue cotton dress
With a pattern of a hundred flowers

Blue cotton
Blue cotton
Blue cotton

BLUES AND KISSES

The moon has packed her bags
And she's caught the evening train
Yes the moon bought a ticket
Gone with the evening train
I'm standing on the pavement
Kisses falling down like rain

Well I'm standing on the pavement
Kisses falling down like rain
Cold wet concrete pavement
Kisses falling down like rain
I'll lay my head on the railway
And wait for the midnight train

Had a dream about some words
Carved on a marble stone
Dreamed I saw some golden words
Carved on a slab of marble stone:
Here lies all the loving
That once upon a time you called your own

Standing on the pavement
Kisses falling down like rain
Cold wet concrete pavement
Kisses falling down like rain
I'll lay my head on the railway
And wait to catch that midnight train

THE PIED PIPER

The show was a last minute decision by the National
Theatre. The director, Alan Cohen, asked me to write it.
There were only three weeks in which to write a first draft,
but it was now or never so it was done. Plot summary and
lyrics first, to give Dominic Muldowney maximum
working time.

I was anxious to know who was going to play the Piper
before I started work on the dialogue and desperate that it
should be Sylvester McCoy, for whom I'd previously
written the parts of Bix Beiderbecke in *Hoagy, Bix and
Wolfgang Beethoven Bunkhaus* and Erik Satie in *Satie Day/
Night*. So I wrote the National a memo entitled Ten
Reasons Why We Need Sylvester McCoy. We got him. He's
a performing genius and I knew that his ideas as well as his
acting would illuminate the play.

The play was constructed to allow room for about 40–50
primary schoolchildren to act with our professionals. They
played rats, drowning happily in the Weser River, at the
end of Act One. In Act Two they made an appearance as
rather downtrodden children, members of Lady Lucy
Saveloy's Remarkable Academy For Children Of
Respectable Folk, wearing dark uniform cloaks. But then,
after taking the side of the Pied Piper, they were magicked
by his *Patchwork Rap*, their cloaks became bright
patchworks and they followed the Piper over the Shivering
Bridge of Dilvergibbon ("where the river down below is
like a silver ribbon"), through the Bottomless Swamp of
Ombroglio (where they met a Welsh monster called The

231

Rampant Umbrage), into the Freezing Forest of Forafter (an encounter with the Iced Knight) and all the way to and into Koppelburg Mountain. The children had a lot to do, acting, singing, dancing of a stompy kind (and some break-dancing for those who wanted to), but they weren't selected for skills – we just took two classes from each school. They were visited and rehearsed in their classrooms by a wonderful team which included Jennie Buckman and Robina Nicolson and then joined the National actors for technical rehearsals before the real thing.

The Pied Piper had two productions at the National. For the second coming I tightened up the script of the first half, which had been difficult. We had to cut down the cast from fifteen to twelve. It was a new cast, retaining only Sylvester (now famous as Doctor Who) and Bill Moody, (for whom I had written the part of Egbert Saveloy).

It played to packed houses of primary school children on weekdays and families at weekends and, the second time around especially, it was about the most rewarding work I ever did for the theatre. It was a long way from Robert Browning's poem, but then his poem was a long way from his source book.

Composer: DOMINIC MULDOWNEY.

Performed: National Theatre (Olivier and Lyttelton) 1986–7, 1987–8.

Published: Oberon Books, 1988.

RIVER WATER

River water
Carry me along
In the shadow
Of the river trees
River water
Cool and green and strong
Waterbirds are playing
On your river breeze

> Where I come from
> I don't remember
> Where I'm going
> I do not care
> River water
> River water
> Carry me along
> To a happy landing
> To a job and lodgings
> Somewhere

River water
Carry me along
Watching fishes
Skim the river bed
River water
Sing your river song
Of the creatures swimming
In your glassy head

> Oh where I come from
> I don't remember
> Where I'm going
> I do not care
> River water
> River water
> Carry me along
> To a happy landing

And some work to do
And a bed to sleep in
And a good hot breakfast
Somewhere

River water
River water

RAT IT UP

C'mon everybody
Slap some grease on those paws
Get some yellow on your teeth
And, uh, sharpen up your claws

There's a whole lot of sausage
We're gonna swallow down
We're going to jump out the sewers
And rock this town

       Cos we're ratting it up
       Yes we're ratting it up
       Well we're ratting it up
       For a ratting good time tonight

Ain't got no compass
You don't need no map
Just follow your snout
Hey, watch out for that trap!

You can take out a poodle
You can beat up a cat
But if you can't lick a ferret
You ain't no kind of rat

       Cos we're ratting it up
       Yes we're ratting it up

Well we're ratting it up
For a ratting good time tonight

Now you can sneak in the henhouse
You can roll out the eggs
But if the farmer comes running
Bite his hairy legs

Check that cheese for poison
Before you eat
Or you'll wind up being served up
As ratburger meat

Cos we're ratting it up
Yes we're ratting it up
Well we're ratting it up
For a ratting good time tonight

This rat was born to rock
This rat was born to roll
I don't give a monkey's
About your pest control

So push off pussy-cat
And push off pup
We're the Rocking Rodents
And we're ratting it up

Yeah we're ratting it up
Yeah we're ratting it up
Well we're ratting it up
For a ratting good time tonight!

PATCHWORK RAP

I'm a touch lazy
Don't like doing much work
But often get the itch
To pitch into some patchwork
It may be a hotchpotch
Like fretwork or such work
Slouching on my couch
I fetch out my patchwork

First I snatch a patch
From the batch in my pouch
But the patch doesn't match
The patches on my patchwork
So I catch another patch
From the batch in my satchel
And this one matches
The patches on my patchwork.
So I take my patch
And attach it with stitches
Patch against patch
Where the patchwork matches
But if it doesn't match
Even after it's attached
Then the mismatched stitch
Has to be detached . . .

You know
I don't like thatchwork
Don't like ditchwork
Only kind I favour
Is my patchwork stitchwork
And soon my patchwork's
Going like clockwork
Sharper than a pitchfork
Neater than brickwork

236

Hotter than a firework
Cooler than a waxwork

So I snatch a patch
From the batch in my pouch
But the patch doesn't match
The patches on my patchwork
So I catch another patch
From the batch in my satchel
And this one matches
The patches on my patchwork.
So I take my patch
And attach it with stitches
Patch against patch
Where the patchwork matches
And I keep on patching
Till everything's matching
And I keep on stitching
Till I've filled up the kitchen
With my rich rich rich rich
Wider than a soccer pitch
Wonderful colour patchwork quilt!
            (Now which stitch is which?)

GORGONZOLA MOON

Gorgonzola Moon
I am shaking like jelly
As your moonbeams turn
The Weser River to cheese

Gorgonzola Moon
You're bright as the telly
You're as good as grime
And you're friendly as fleas

I take one sniff of you
And I'm ready to take a chance
Just one sweet sniff of you
And I'm singing a song
Another sniff of you
And I'm ready to break-a dance
When I sniff a whiff
Of your wonderful pong

Gorgonzola Moon
Shine down on my belly
Let your perfume fly
On the riverside breeze

Gorgonzola Moon
You're so beautifully smelly
That I'm glad to drown
Down in the river of cheese

Yes I'm happy to drown
Going down going down
Happy to drown
Down in the river
In the river of melted Gorgonzola cheese

GONE MISSING

Where have our children gone?
Where have our children gone?
Lost in the forest
Or drowned in the ditches?
Eaten by lions
Or stolen by witches?
Gone missing, gone missing, gone missing.

Where have our children gone?
Where have our children gone?
Captured by giants
Or buried in blizzards?
Swallowed for breakfast
By man-eating lizards?
Gone missing, gone missing, gone missing.

Where have our children gone?
Where have our children gone?
Bitten by vampires
Or flattened by tractors?
Sunk in a swamp or
Run off to be actors?
Gone missing, gone missing, gone missing.

SECRET COUNTRY

there is no money
so there's no crime
there are no watches
'cos there's no time
it's a good country
it's a secret country
and it's your country and mine

if you need something
you make it there
and we have plenty
for we all share
it's a kind country
it's a secret country
and it's your country and mine

there are no cages
there is no zoo
but the free creatures
come and walk with you
it's a strange country
it's a secret country
and it's your country and mine

there are no prisons
there are no poor
there are no weapons
there is no war
it's a safe country
it's a secret country
and it's your country and mine

and in that country
grows a great tree
and it's called Freedom
and it's fruit is free
in that blue country
in that warm country
in that loving country
in that ragamuffin country
in that secret country
which is your country and mine

THE LAST WILD WOOD IN SECTOR 88

It's a 35 minute opera for children. It's about some kids
who are playing in a wood when they overhear a group of
surveyors talking about the destruction of the wood to
make way for various profitable schemes. The kids invade
a local inquiry but get turned out. In the end they win by
consciously copying the methods of the women in Sri
Lanka – hugging the trees and refusing to let go when the
axes arrive to chop down the wood they love.

Guy Woolfenden invited me to write the piece with him.
I based it on my own love for Rainbow Woods in Combe
Down, near Bath, where I was evacuated to in World War
Two. I told this to the children who performed the piece in
Rugby and one of them came up to me afterwards and said
he goes on holiday in Bath and loves Rainbow Woods and
they are still standing and still beautiful.

Composer: GUY WOOLFENDEN.

Performed: Rugby Music Centre, 1987.

Published: Ariel Music, Sibford Ferris, Banbury,
Oxfordshire OX15 5RG.

THE KIDS OBJECT

KIDS:
Well, it's our wild wood
And it's always been here.
Yes, here it's been
For thousands of year.

FUDGE:
I come to the wild wood
To watch the butterflies.
I want to be a butterfly expert
Curing butterfly diseases.

JENNY:
I come to the wild wood
On my BMX.
I like to bump over the roots
And stuntjump over stumps of trees.

SCOTT:
I come to the wild wood
To play my trumpet
And only the rabbits
Ever complain.

BRENDAN:
I come to the wild wood
To climb the trees.
I like to be as near the sky
As I possibly can.

HELEN:
I come to the wild wood
To watch the badgers.

TOMMY:
I come to the wild wood
Because I like it being green.

ALEX:
I come to the wild wood
To find the buried treasure
Of Stubbly Jacobson
The famous smuggler.

SUE:
I come to the wild wood
With my collie-dog Dumper.
He likes to have a dig
And he's very fond of trees.

SCRUFFO: I come to the wild wood
                Because my mother says I mustn't.
                You can get really well scruffed up
                In the wild wood and I love being
                scruffy.

MAUD: I come to the wild wood
                When my dad gets drunk.

KIDS: And it's our wild wood
                And it's always been here.
                Yes, here it's been
                For thousands of year.

                Well, it's our wild wood
                And our dads and our mams
                First wheeled us out here
                In pushchairs and prams

                To this wild wood
                Where we yell and we bike
                And we build and we climb
                As we woody well like.

                Yes, it's our wild wood
                And it's always been here
                And it'll keep growing
                For another thousand year.

GREEN

Green shining
Green shifting
Green sunshine
Green

Green giving
Green swaying
Green being
Green growing
Green

Thrush home
Squirrel village
Red ant motorway
Caterpillar skyscraper
Sparrow world

Star net
Sunlight drinker
Rainfall welcomer
Openhanded snowfall catcher
Wooden world

Green shining
Green shifting
Green shadows
Green sunshine
Green

Green living
Green playing
Green sighing
Green singing
Green

WE

Not to be confused with *US*. It's a future musical based on Zamyatin's great novel. I'd dreamed of it for years and finally Richard Peaslee got the piece commissioned by the Minnesota Opera Company, thus buying us time in which to write.

First we laboriously mapped out a detailed story-line, using a complex system of filing cards all over the floor, and decided where songs were necessary. Then we spent two fevered, happy weeks in the Peaslees' wooden house in Index, Washington, with a rocky river in front of us, a towering forest behind us and mountains all around. All day I'd work at lyrics in one room, Dick would write tunes at the piano in the next and his wife Dixie would paint in a third. After work we'd hike up and down mountains at a ridiculous pace and then feed at the Gold Bar Diner. It was a good way to work, and the forest which lies outside the city of glass in *We* became the North-Western forest we walked in every day and details from that forest spilled into the lyrics.

The next stage was the dialogue, which I wrote in Deya, Majorca, in between swims. As I write we are still waiting to hear from the first two theatres we've shown the show to, but three of the songs have already been heard in *Love Songs of World War Three* at the National, where Patsy Rowlands gave a beautiful performance of *Lilies of the Valley*.

Composer: RICHARD PEASLEE.

Performed: In the future.

WE

We!
Who can be stronger than We?
We!
Who can last longer than We!
We won't go under
Not We!
We know the wonder of We!
It's so fine to be
A unit of We!
Yes! We! Yes! We! Yes! We!

We are the Numbers of the One State.
We are a thousand strong.
We wear our numbers and we feel great
As we sing, swinging along:
Hey take a good look at us!
We are marching from minus to plus!
Yes! We! Yes! We! Yes! We! Yes! We!

LOVERS COME, LOVERS GO

Lovers come
Lovers go
And the world spins on
Step inside
For a look
At the days that have gone.
Lovers come
Lovers go
And the clock moves too fast,
So turn back its hands
Till they're touching the past.

You may win,
You may lose,
Only one thing I know –
As the world spins in space
Lovers come
Lovers go.

HIS HANDS

I see his hands.
I see the back of his hands.
I touch his hands.
I touch the back of his careful hands.
I stroke his hands,
The swirling hairs on the back of his hands.

> When I take his face in my hands
> He closes his eyelids,
> Then he gives his tentative smile,
> Kisses both my palms.
> When we love we're melting away,
> Like a crystal dissolving,
> Like a pear-tree blossoming white –
> Darling, never forget . . .

My lovely moon calf,
I set out to fool you,
To steal your secrets
By pretending to love.
Now I'm the moon calf –
I'm no longer fooling
And the only secret
Is the truth of my love.

I see your hands.
I see the back of your hands.
I touch your hands.
I touch the back of your careful hands.
I stroke your hands,
The swirling hairs on the back of your hands,
The swirling hairs on the back of your hands . . .

THE HYMN OF UNANIMITY

Every morning
At the same moment
We arise as one
Every morning
At the same moment
March to work as one
Every morning
At the same moment
Do our work as one
Every morning
At the same moment
Eat our food as one
Wonderful, wonderful
        One.

One State
One Thought
One Great
Design
One fine
Exact
And straight
Straight line.

248

One Heart
One Hand
One Might –
-y Mind.
One State
One Thought
One Great
Design.

LAMENT FOR THE JAZZ MAKERS

As I was sitting all alone
Death called me on the telephone
I said: I'm sorry, I'm not free.
The fear of death is haunting me.

Death is the cop who can't be bought.
You always think you won't be caught,
Until you're busted, finally –
The fear of death is eating me.

Death grabs the young cat by the neck –
He stomped upon Bix Biederbecke
Whose cornet rung so silvery.
The fear of death is shaking me.

And death has locked up Lester Young
And Billie Holiday who sung
Her beaten-up black poetry.
The fear of death is clutching me.

Tatum, Django, Charlie Mingus,
Death snapped off their cunning fingers
Like twigs from some old apple tree.
The fear of death is breaking me.

Death took the great Duke Ellington
And wore him down to skin and bone
For all his generosity.
The fear of death is taunting me.

Louis, Mama Yancey, Dinah,
Bessie Smith and Big Joe Turner
All work in death's bad factory.
The fear of death is chilling me.

He breathed in air, he breathed out light,
Charlie Parker was my delight
But Bird was cut down cruelly.
The fear of death is touching me.

And we must all of us go dwell
In Death's enormous Black Hotel.
At least we'll have good company –
The fear of death is killing me.

APESHIT

The cigarette took my nerve-ends
And it cooled them into a blur.
The alcohol slammed my brain-cells
Till I couldn't tell me from her.
I was jumping on a volcano.
I was crawling in an ancient tomb.
I was everywhere!
I was covered in hair!
Then I shouted: "Back to the womb!"

> I went Apeshit
> With my eyeballs burning
> Apeshit

250

With my buttocks churning
    Apeshit
With my toes and teeth
Sometimes on my top
Sometimes underneath
    Apeshit

Inside of a giant eggshell,
And attempting to break out
I wanted to catch a sidewalk
But I'd swallowed a magic trout.
I was up to my eyes in bosom.
I was down on my luck in Hell.
I was in Bulgaria
Getting much hairier!
So I gave an engineer's yell –

I went Apeshit
With my kneecaps banging
    Apeshit
With my conkers clanging
    Apeshit
With an Apeshit mind
Sometimes in front
And sometimes from behind

    Apeshit
You can call me Jimmy
    Apeshit
O gimme gimme gimme
    Apeshit
      Holy
    Apeshit
      I got
    Apeshit
      Give me
    Apeshit
      Happy

                    Apeshit
                            Darling
                    Apeshit
                    Apeshit
A P E S H I T ! ! !

LILIES OF THE VALLEY

In this clever city
Built of glass and steel
Everything's so perfect
That it seems unreal
But I found a corner
Where there's mud and sand
And I brought a present
From that patch of land –

                    Lilies of the Valley
                    Gentle green and white
                    Lilies of the Valley
                    Cast a little light.
                    They tremble in
                    The stillest air
                    But they stand straight and true –
                    Lilies of the Valley
                    Lilies of the Valley
                    For you.

And I see a valley
Where a river flows
Wild and strong and rocky
Fed by mountain snows
And I see a forest
By the river shore

And I see a shining
On the forest floor –

Lilies of the Valley
Gentle green and white
Lilies of the Valley
Cast a little light.
They tremble in
The stillest air
But they stand straight and true –
Lilies of the Valley
Lilies of the Valley
For you.

GATHER TOGETHER

Gather together
The snow-drinking waterfalls
Gather together
The tears of the pine
The glassy-winged insects
The woodpecker's drum

Gather together
The soft-springing forest floor
Gather together
The lumbering bear
Inflammable maples
The spears of the sun

Gather together
The cry of the falling tree
Gather together
The apple-green pond

The leap of the squirrel
The patience of stones

Gather together
The snaggle-toothed undergrowth
Gather together
The spite of the storm
The acrobat swallows
The glaring of bones

Gather together
The green-fountain conifers
Gather together
The choir of the wolves
The strong breath of mushrooms
The butterwort flowers

Gather together
The shouting of cataracts
Gather together
The racket of rooks
The songs of the forest
The forest is ours

THE HEN AND THE EAGLE

Sanity is stagnant
Madness can jump
Oneday noon to sevenday night
Sanity's the sanitary
Padded cell
Madness is the bundle of dynamite.

> I want to fly through the roof of the sky
> Not flap around a chickenwire pen

A hen is a logical eagle
An eagle is a crazy hen

Sanity's the One State's Cancerous growth
Suffocating natural life.
Impulse is the surgeon who can
Cut it out
Madness is the name of his shining knife

I want to fly through the roof of the sky
Not flap around a chickenwire pen
A hen is a logical eagle
An eagle is a crazy hen

Sanity's a giant
Adding machine
Counts your heartbeats while you're at work
Madness is the percolating
Heat of love
Magically helping us to go berserk –

I want to fly through the roof of the sky
Not flap around a chickenwire pen
A hen is a logical eagle
An eagle is a crazy hen

EVENINGS OF FIRE AND SNOW

Don't look so worried
I understand
Let me touch your forehead
With my freckled hand
Won't you sit beside me
For a little while?
It would satisfy me

Just to see you smile

> I'm transparent
> Look into me
> Look at my childish heart's
> Simplicity
> Whiteness shining
> And a crimson glow
> Heat and coldness
> Fire and snow

And if you'll allow me we will know
Evenings of fire and snow

Don't want to own you
I'm happy just to share
It's a joy to know you
Know you know I care.
Won't you let me love you
On this sunset day?
Smiling when you leave me,
I will only say –

> I'm transparent
> Look into me
> Look at my childish heart's
> Simplicity
> Whiteness shining
> And a crimson glow
> Heat and coldness
> Fire and snow

And if you'll allow me we will know
Evenings of fire and snow.

LOVE SONGS OF WORLD WAR THREE

Jan Younghusband of the National Theatre needed a show
to fill two nights in the Cottesloe Theatre and asked me if I
could think of one. It seemed like a good opportunity to
try out a songbook show, using some of the cast of *The Pied
Piper*, which was running at that time.

The budget was miniscule – we could only afford one
pianist, three actors, a director and myself. I decided to get
an extra actor by becoming the director. To my surprise
the first four overworked actors I approached agreed to be
in the show. My old friend Sylvester McCoy, Patsy
Rowlands of variety and *Carry On* fame, Diane Bull who's
one of the funniest actresses alive and Brian Hibbard,
formerly the lead singer with The Flying Pickets. Matthew
Scott, whom I'd worked with on *Animal Farm* came in as
pianist, MD, arranger and general rock. Three of the stage
management team from the *Piper* joined us and everyone
worked like crazy in the few hours we could grab for
rehearsals.

The first rehearsal was nearly a disaster. The actors had
played two shows that day and were ready for home.
Wanting to get their reactions as quickly as possible to the
maximum amount of material, I played them tapes of
approximately 40 songs. I'm sorry, I'm really sorry.

Soon we had it down to about 32 songs linked mainly by
commentary and a few poems by me. We played on the set
of David Edgar's *Entertaining Strangers* – the audience
sitting on cushions on a sloping grassy hill. Our
background was the Jungle of Eden screens made by Jenni

257

Gregory for *C'Mon Everybody*. Songs came from *Tyger*, *Marat/Sade*, *US*, *Animal Farm*, *The Pied Piper*, *Mind Your Head* and other shows. The choreography was rugged but right. I was allowed to sing the Soldier's part in Bad Friday – directors can do anything. I was scared silly but the Cottesloe was packed both nights. We only had three reviews – one vicious and two marvellous.

I came to write the ballad *Victor Jara of Chile* because, after the fascist coup in Chile, three refugees arrived and stayed at my house. They were Joan Jara and her two young daughters, Mandy and Manuela. Joan was married to Victor Jara, who had been killed in the first days of the coup. We talked about Chile, about how Victor died and then we talked, at length, about how Victor lived. Joan was going to meetings every night telling his story and the story of Chile. We wanted to find other ways of doing this. The BBC at this time had decided to run a "topical drama" slot, so we offered the idea of a play about Victor's life. They commissioned it, I wrote two drafts. The play was announced and, even before it was written, was attacked in the press as being predictably left-wing, given the subject and my track record. But the BBC stood up to pressure. They accepted the play, but, in the same phone call, they postponed it indefinitely. Two months had gone by since Victor's death and they thought it was no longer topical.

I wrote my ballad to a tune by Woody Guthrie called *Dear Mrs Roosevelt*. Joan approved and I sent it to Arlo Guthrie, hoping he'd sing it. He set it to a new tune of his own and recorded it.

Composers: ARLO GUTHRIE and ROBYN ARCHER (*The Biggest Bang*).

Performed: Cottesloe Theatre, National Theatre, 1988.

VICTOR JARA OF CHILE

Victor Jara of Chile
Lived like a shooting star
He fought for the people of Chile
With his songs and his guitar

And his hands were gentle
His hands were strong

Victor Jara was a peasant
Worked from a few years old
He sat upon his father's plough
And watched the earth unfold

And his hands were gentle
His hands were strong

When the neighbours had a wedding
Or one of their children died
His mother sang all night for them
With Victor by her side

And his hands were gentle
His hands were strong

He grew to be a fighter
Against the people's wrongs
He listened to their grief and joy
And turned them into songs

And his hands were gentle
His hands were strong

He sang about the copper miners
And those who work the land
He sang about the factory workers
And they knew he was their man

And his hands were gentle
His hands were strong

He campaigned for Allende
Working night and day
He sang: Take hold of your brother's hand
The future begins today

And his hands were gentle
His hands were strong

The bloody generals seized Chile
They arrested Victor then
They caged him in a stadium
With five thousand frightened men

And his hands were gentle
His hands were strong

Victor stood in the stadium
His voice was brave and strong
He sang for his fellow-prisoners
Till the guards cut short his song

And his hands were gentle
His hands were strong

They broke the bones in both his hands
They beat his lovely head
They tore him with electric shocks
And then they shot him dead

And his hands were gentle
His hands were strong

And now the generals rule Chile
And the British have their thanks
For they rule with Hawker Hunters
And they rule with Chieftain tanks

And his hands were gentle
His hands were strong

Victor Jara of Chile
Lived like a shooting star

He fought for the people of Chile
With his songs and his guitar

And his hands were gentle
His hands were strong

His hands were gentle
His hands were strong

THE BIGGEST BANG

We done it with pictures we done it with words
pounds and dollars and all
With hoare-belisha beacons and thunderbirds
at the money-fuckers ball

Grabbed 'em by the scruff of the groin
pounds and dollars and all
pumped 'em full of the slippery coin
at the money-fuckers ball

Fifteen suicides screwing all night
pounds and dollars and all
rolled in a ball down a mountain of shite
at the money-fuckers' ball

Money money money money come in a shower
pounds and dollars and all
give me a stand like the Post Office Tower
at the money-fuckers' ball

Fucked the Bank of England and caught the pox
pounds and dollars and all
jumped the Atlantic and buggered Fort Knox
at the money-fuckers' ball

One blind bankrupt couldn't get a screw
pounds and dollars and all
tossed himself off with an IOU
at the money-fuckers' ball

JUST A LITTLE TOO LOUD

The boys in the bar are easy
Yeah the boys in the bar are fine
Not much in our pockets
Not much on our minds
You smile at us and we nod at you
But you better not go too far
Just a little too loud
And a little too near the bar

>   Now the businessman from Boston
>   Stayed with us for around three hours
>   Talking up the price of real estate
>   Swallowing whisky sours
>   They found sugar in the gastank
>   Of his fancy German car
>   Just a little too loud
>   And a little too near the bar

Just a little too loud for the country
Just a little too loud for us
You don't need to order cocktails
Like you're flagging down a Greyhound bus
You smile at us and we nod at you
But you better not go too far
Just a little too loud
And a little too near the bar

Middle-age college couple
Two of them dressed in green
Recording our conversation
On a little-bitty tape machine
Well that tape machine and their spectacles too
Got vanished in a barrel of tar
Just a little too loud
And a little too near the bar

Just a little too loud for the country
Just a little too loud for us
You don't need to order cocktails
Like you're flaggin' down a Greyhound bus
You smile at us and we nod at you
But you better not go too far
Just a little too loud
And a little too near the bar

We had some barefoot surfers
In their sawn-off raggy jeans
And we taught those barefoot surfers
Exactly what barefoot means
Cos they sneered at Jeannie's accent
And they laughed at Billy's scar
Just a little too loud
And a little too near the bar

Just a little too loud for the country
Just a little too loud for us
You don't need to order cocktails
Like you're flaggin' down a Greyhound bus
You smile at us and we nod at you
But you better not go too far
Just a little too loud
And a little too near the bar

Also by **Adrian Mitchell**
and published by Allison & Busby:

FOR BEAUTY DOUGLAS
Collected Poems 1953–79
Illustrated by Ralph Steadman

'I doubt if Mitchell would thank me for saying it as he would
not make such distinctions, but in any given time there are
only a few master-poets. Ted Hughes is one, a weighty,
gloomy master, a dark master-poet. Another, brighter, more
inventive, travelling the same heights and same darknesses
yet always shining and, for me, with a greater sympathy and
at an opposite pole, is Mitchell. His influence on the early
work of myself and my contemporaries, both as performer
and poet-inventor, has been considerable. It is both a debt
we are proud to acknowledge and a gift we are glad to have
received' – Brian Patten

ON THE BEACH AT CAMBRIDGE
New Poems

'Adrian Mitchell is no more naïve than Stevie Smith, but
like her he has the innocence of his own experience . . . real
inner freedom and the courage of his own music. Among all
the voices of the Court, a voice as welcome as Lear's fool . . .
Humour that can stick deep and stay funny' – Ted Hughes

THE BODYGUARD
A Novel

'A forceful, gripping and distinguished piece of work. It is
something of a tour de force' – *The Listener*

'A model of sustained inventiveness' – *New Statesman*

IF YOU SEE ME COMIN'
A Novel

'Brilliantly edgy first novel . . . funny, exciting, desperate and
serious. Don't miss it' – *Spectator*

'The way in which an imaginative concern with our society's
cruelties can drive a man towards madness is here movingly
described' – *Times Literary Supplement*